MUSEUM JOBS FROM A–Z

What They Are, How to Prepare, and Where to Find Them

**Revised and Edited by
G. W. Bates**

D1115998

**Batax Museum Publishing
2051 Wheeler Lane
Jacksonville, FL 32259**

Publisher's Cataloging in Publication
(Prepared by Quality Books Inc.)

Bates, G.W., 1955-
    Museum jobs from A-Z: what they are, how to prepare, and where to find them / revised and edited by G.W. Bates.
    p. cm.
    ISBN 0-9629759-4-X

    1. Museums--Vocational guidance--United States.   I. Title. II. Title: Museum jobs from A to Z.

AM11.B38 1994   069'.023
                            QBI93-22068

TABLE OF
CONTENTS

Preface v

I. Occupations 1

II. Learning Opportunities 131

III. Recommended Reading 135

IV. Index by Job Title 136

PREFACE

The occupational descriptions contained in this volume, having been compiled from a number of different sources, describe the individual occupations in general terms. Consequently, no description can be expected to coincide exactly with a specific job in a particular establishment or locality. To be more useful, the descriptions should be supplemented by local information about specific jobs in the community.

ANIMAL KEEPER

OCCUPATIONAL STATEMENT

Feeds, waters, and cleans quarters of animals in zoo: Prepares food for charges by chopping or grinding meat, fish, fruit, or vegetables, mixing prepared dry or liquid commercial feeds, or unbaling forage grasses. Adds vitamins or medication to feed, as prescribed by veterinarian. Fills water containers and places food in cages at specified times. Cleans animal quarters by raking, hosing, scrubbing, and disinfecting quarters as needed. Observes animals to detect indications of illness such as changes in appetite, disposition, or habits, or changes in physical appearance or excreta. Transfers animals from one to another enclosure, for such purposes as breeding, giving birth, rearrangement of exhibits or shipping. Sets temperature and humidity controls of quarters according to instructions of veterinarian or Animal Keeper, Head. Answers visitors' questions concerning animals' habits or zoo operations. Bathes and grooms animals used in programs. May assist Zoo Veterinarian in providing preventive or therapeutic treatment to animals. May assist Animal Trainer or instructor in presentation of programs, shows, or lectures. May assist maintenance staff in cleaning of zoo facilities. May be designated according to animals cared for, as bear keeper, elephant keeper, or according to species, as bird keeper, mammal keeper.

EDUCATION, TRAINING, AND EXPERIENCE

The hiring requirement most stressed by zoos is experience in handling, feeding, and breeding animals. This experience may have been acquired through work on a farm or ranch, or through training in animal husbandry, veterinary science, or other formal courses. Some zoos have cooperative work/study programs for keepers (Intern Zoo Keeper) with local high schools, and a few junior colleges offer a curriculum leading to an associate's degree in zoo keeping. Many zoos hire keeper trainees, who receive on-the-job training to learn all of the keepers' functions and responsibilities. Educational hiring requirements vary from zoo to zoo. Although most ask for at least a high school education, many do not have any stated academic requirements, especially if an applicant has had a farm background and is well versed in methods of caring for various domestic animals. Many zoos discourage college graduates with degrees in zoology or one of its specialties (herpetology, ornithotomy) from seeking jobs as keepers as a way of entering zoo work; however, others have policies which permit or encourage such applications. The only way to

1

find out about hiring requirements of individual zoos is to question personnel associated with them.

HELPFUL PERSONAL CHARACTERISTICS

Animal Keepers should, naturally, enjoy working with animals. Aside from liking them, they should also feel a sense of responsibility for their well-being, and be willing to perform the routine, sometimes unpleasant, duties necessary to feed and care for animals and their quarters. Since veterinarians and other administrative personnel depend on keepers to notice indications of illness in animals. Keepers must learn how to recognize these indications and report them immediately.

PHYSICAL DEMANDS AND ENVIRONMENTAL CONDITIONS

This is active work, demanding the ability to move quickly and agilely when cleaning quarters, preparing food, and handling animals. Strength requirements vary according to the kind of animal being kept; for instance, pushing and pulling large animals such as elephants or hippopotami requires much more physical strength and endurance than handling prairie dogs or snakes. However, agility is needed by all keepers, and most zoos require applicants to pass physical examinations. These are given to test applicants, not only for strength and agility, but also for freedom from disease because human illnesses can often be passed on to animals. Anyone wanting to be an Animal Keeper should realize that working with wild animals involves some danger. Even though they have been caged for months or years, animals, just like people, can lose their tempers, become irritated because of illness, or otherwise revert to their wild behavior; keepers must become accustomed to constant caution, even after long experience.

WHERE TO FIND THESE JOBS

Animal Keepers' jobs are located in large and small zoos all over the country. Also, some natural history or general museums maintain collections of live animals and employ keepers.

OPPORTUNITIES FOR EMPLOYMENT AND PROMOTION

Zoos hire more Animal Keepers than any other classification so, depending on employee turnover, there are more likely to be openings in these positions than in others. About half of the zoos are municipally operated, and applications for employment are accepted through municipal civil service offices. At other zoos, including some operated by cities, application is made directly at the zoo office. Advancement from keeper jobs varies according to both worker qualifications and zoo operating policies. In zoos that accept college-trained people as keepers, advancement to Curator or instructor positions is possible; for keepers with only high school background, advancement to head keeper, Animal Trainer, or Animal Nurse is possible and, in a few cases, these workers can get into curatorial or other more advanced work. In some cities, zoo employees belong to unions, usually those that represent government workers, and advancement to other jobs is attained by bidding on these when openings occur.

ANIMAL KEEPER, HEAD

OCCUPATIONAL STATEMENT

Supervises and coordinates activities of workers engaged in care and exhibition of birds and animals at establishments such as zoos or circuses: Observes animals to detect signs of illness and consults with veterinarian (medical ser.) to determine type of medication or treatment required. Inspects cages, grottos, and pens for cleanliness and structural defects. Assigns workers to various tasks, and oversees treatment, preparation of food, feeding of animals, and maintenance and repair of animal quarters. Specifies type of animals to exhibit in zoo and location of exhibit according to weather, animal behavior characteristics, and animal physical condition. Recommends or initiates personnel actions, such as promotions, transfers, discharges, and disciplinary measures. Analyzes and resolves work problems, and assists workers in solving problems. Maintains time and personnel records. Supervises or participates in moving of animals to new quarters or in crating or uncrating animals for shipment or display. May prepare requisitions for animal foods, supplies, and equipment. May hire, train, or discharge workers. May give lectures to public to stimulate interest in animals. May be employed by aquarium, and be known as aquarist, head.

EDUCATION, TRAINING, AND EXPERIENCE

Most Animal Keepers, Head, have advanced to their positions after several years of experience in the care and feeding of animals, usually at the same establishment. High school graduation is usually required for hiring consideration. The Head Animal Keeper may supervise the entire keeper staff at a small zoo, while a head keeper at a large zoo may be in charge of, for instance, only keepers assigned to caring for primates or reptiles. In these larger zoos, advancement is usually from a less responsible to a more responsible supervisory position.

Many zoos and aquariums are operated by cities or other regional government bodies, and applicants may have to take civil service tests, in addition to having the specified amount of experience required for application for these positions.

3

HELPFUL PERSONAL CHARACTERISTICS

Animal Keepers, Head, must be able to organize their own work schedules and those of others, make decisions regarding the assignment and evaluation of duties performed by subordinate workers, and retain the interest in caring for animals which they had as keepers.

They should also have numerical and clerical aptitude, to maintain personnel time and performance records, prepare requisitions for feed and other materials, and, in some establishments, maintain financial records of the display operations of the zoo.

PHYSICAL DEMANDS AND ENVIRONMENTAL CONDITIONS

This is an indoor-outdoor occupation whose physical demands vary from light to heavy, depending on the responsibilities of individual positions. Animal Keepers, Head, do much desk work—maintaining records, requisitioning supplies, or preparing reports—but they also spend a good deal of time out of doors visiting animal display and animal quarters and evaluating the work performance of subordinates. In some zoos, head keepers also have the responsibility for the direct care of certain animals, so that they must be in the same excellent physical condition required of keepers.

Although head keepers are occasionally subject to the same hazards and unpleasant environmental conditions encountered by keepers, adjustment to these would have taken place by the time promotion to these positions occurred, so that their presence is not really a significant factor in the job.

WHERE TO FIND THESE JOBS

Head keepers are employed by zoos and aquariums all over the country. Small zoos employ only one person in this capacity, but large zoos may have as many as 10 or 12 persons in these supervisory roles.

OPPORTUNITIES FOR EMPLOYMENT AND PROMOTION

It would be extremely rare for a person without previous keeper experience, almost always at the same establishment, to be hired as a Head Animal Keeper. Employment opportunities are for all practical purposes, limited to persons currently employed, who possess the leadership and organizational characteristics needed for supervisory work.

In large zoos, head keepers can advance from minor to major supervisory positions. In a few institutions, these workers may advance to curatorial or administrative jobs without further education.

4

ANIMAL NURSE

OCCUPATIONAL STATEMENT

Cares for newborn and young animals in exhibit area or zoo nursery: Prepares liquid formula, cereal, and other foods for young animals, according to directions of Zoo Veterinarian, and prepares standard diet foods for mothers of newborn animals according to requirements of species. Fills sterilized nursing bottles with formula and feeds animals which have been orphaned or deserted, or which require food in addition to that provided by mother. Maintains close watch over newborn animals to note indications of abnormality or disease, and notifies Zoo Veterinarian when such indications are evident. Periodically conducts physical examination of young animals, performing such tasks as taking temperatures, blood pressure, and pulse rate, and weighing and measuring animals. Maintains records of animals' weight, size, and physical condition to be used in zoo's account of animals born in captivity. As directed by Zoo Veterinarian, adjusts instruments which control temperature and humidity of animal nursery or exhibit area to maintain environmental conditions according to needs of species. When assigned to young animal exhibit area, sets up, or directs others to set up, special facilities, such as infra-red light standards, cribs, or feeding devices required for the care of young animals on display. Explains care and feeding procedures of various young animals to visitors and answers questions concerning animals' native habitat, breeding habits, and other factors. Observes children petting or feeding animals in designated area, and cautions children against activities that might be harmful to animals.

EDUCATION, TRAINING, AND EXPERIENCE

In most zoos, these positions are filled by persons who have had experience as Animal Keepers, usually at the same establishment. They are given 6 to 8 weeks training in the special techniques used in caring for young animals and in the methods of acquiring information about the in- and out-of-captivity living habits of animals on display.

HELPFUL PERSONAL CHARACTERISTICS

To perform this job well. The Animal Nurse should have all of the qualities needed by Animal Keepers plus the ability to meet and speak easily to the public Since young animals must frequently, literally, be treated like babies, they should enjoy holding them, feeding them, and comforting them when necessary. They should also be responsible enough to follow directions closely when mixing and measuring formu-

5

las and other food, and when recording information to be used in zoo reports.

PHYSICAL DEMANDS AND ENVIRONMENTAL CONDITIONS

Jobs as Animal Nurse are less physically demanding than those of Animal Keepers because cleaning quarters and carrying large containers of feed are tasks performed by other workers, and animals handled are not likely to attack. The typical work site is the clean, well-lit, and ventilated zoo nursery and/or the section of the zoo's exhibit area (often called a children's zoo) where many young animals are quartered. The job makes no unusual physical demands on workers, and there is little risk of injury.

WHERE TO FIND THESE JOBS

Jobs as Animal Nurse are found in many zoos.

OPPORTUNITIES FOR EMPLOYMENT AND PROMOTION

New employees are seldom, hired for this position. Persons who think they would enjoy this kind of work should try to find jobs as Animal Keepers at a zoo which has this kind of facility, and explain that they are interested in becoming Animal Nurses. There is little opportunity for advancement to higher level jobs from this one, without the educational background needed for curatorial work. In some zoos, Animal Nurses can become instructors or head keepers without further education. The experience of meeting and speaking to the public, acquired in the job of Animal Nurse, could provide valuable background for advancement to these higher level jobs.

ANIMAL TRAINER

OCCUPATIONAL STATEMENT

Trains animals to obey commands, compete in shows, or perform tricks to entertain audiences: Evaluates animal to determine temperament, ability, and aptitude for training. Conducts training program to develop desired behavior. May organize format of show. May conduct show. May cue or signal animal during performance. May rehearse animal according to script for motion picture or television film or stage or circus program. May train guard dog to protect property. May teach guide dog and master to function as team. May feed, exercise, and give general care to animal. Trainers are identified according to specific animal trained. May be designated head animal trainer or senior animal trainer when directing activities of other workers.

6

EDUCATION, EXPERIENCE, AND TRAINING

Hiring requirements for these jobs vary according to the individual zoos and aquariums where they are found. In many establishments, only persons with recent experience as Animal Keepers or Aquarists are employed as trainers, because the care and feeding of the animals is an important part of most of their duties. Some establishments require that persons in these positions-have training in animal psychology, in addition to work experience caring for animals in a zoo, circus, or the entertainment field. Very few establishments hire people as trainers without assigning them first to jobs in animal caretaking. Because trainers must not only evaluate the individual animals' temperament, intelligence, and trainability, but also, literally, make friends with them in order to gain their confidence and establish rapport, the animal caretaking experience is imperative.

Experiences such as training guide dogs or guard dogs or conducting an animal act are helpful for hiring consideration, but even persons with this kind of background must start out caring for animals, rather than beginning to train them immediately.

HELPFUL PERSONAL CHARACTERISTICS

Animal Trainers should, of course, be interested in working with animals. However, they should also be able to relate to them on an individual basis, treating each animal in the manner most effective for the successful execution of the training program.

Animal training consists, primarily, of repetition and reward; persons in this kind of work must be exceptionally patient and willing to spend long hours going over and over routines with their charges, rewarding them with treats when they successfully perform a trick, but refraining from any form of punishment when they fail.

Animal Trainers must be perceptive enough to recognize potentially trainable animals, as well as those that cannot be trained. They must be able to exercise the authority needed to keep performing animals under control without raising their voices or resorting to physical force, and to stay calm when confronted with the stress situations which are always possible when dealing with wild animals.

Trainers who do their own announcing should have good stage presence as well as the ability to speak well before an audience.

PHYSICAL DEMANDS AND ENVIRONMENTAL CONDITIONS

Except in areas with warm weather year round, most zoo and aquarium shows are seasonal beginning in April or May, and continuing until mid-autumn. Trainers usually work indoors during the winter months to choose, become acquainted with, and train the animals for warm weather performances.

Most work of this kind does not require any more physical strength than that needed by keepers but, depending on the kind of animal involved, most trainers need better than average physical agility. Persons who train such aquatic performers as dolphins and seals should feel at ease working around, in, and under water.

WHERE TO FIND THESE JOBS

Animal Trainers work in zoos and aquariums all over the country. Most of these institutions present some sort of animal show, and many of the larger establishments may have shows featuring a number of different kinds of animals. Elephants, apes, lions, dolphins, porpoises, seals, and birds are among the species most often trained to perform and, generally, institutions that have the largest numbers of these animals are the ones most likely to present such shows. Animal Trainers also work at theme-type amusement parks, oceanariums, or museums that have incorporated live animal displays or aquariums into their organization.

OPPORTUNITIES FOR EMPLOYMENT AND PROMOTION

There are limited opportunities for work in this field. Individual establishments employ only one to 10 persons as trainers, and most of these have been promoted to their jobs from positions as Animal Keepers. As zoos and aquariums expand their operations, more may initiate the practice of providing animal shows as attractions, especially in cases where they are permitted to charge admission and thereby add to the institution's revenue. This could result in a few more openings for trainers than those now available through normal personnel turnover. Persons who think they would like to do this kind of work should apply for jobs as keepers at establishments which now present this kind of entertainment, and let supervisory personnel know of both their interest in, and preparation for, jobs as Animal Trainers.

Summer jobs as trainers are often available to students who have had some education in animal psychology, plus previous experience caring for the species to be trained. These are most likely to be located at the large amusement or theme parks scattered throughout the country. There is often heavy competition for these jobs, so persons interested should be well qualified and apply for the positions early in the year.

Advancement to supervisory positions is possible in institutions employing several Animal Trainers.

AQUARIST

OCCUPATIONAL STATEMENT

Attends fish and other aquatic life in aquarium exhibits: Prepares food and feeds fish according to schedule. Cleans tanks and removes algae from tank windows. Attends to aquatic plants and decorations in displays. Collects and compares water samples to color coded chart for acid analysis and monitors thermometers to ascertain water temperature. Adjusts thermostat and adds chemicals to water to maintain specified water conditions. Observes fish to detect disease and injuries, reports conditions to supervisor, and treats fish according to instructions. May fire sedation gun and assist crew expedition members in collection of aquatic life.

EDUCATION, TRAINING, AND EXPERIENCE

Most employers require that Aquarists have at least a high school education, and some prefer to hire persons who have had a year or two of college, with courses in marine biology or other sciences. Work experience in a fish hatchery or other organization where contact with and care of aquatic creatures is carried on is desirable, but not necessary. The successful raising of tropical fish, turtles, or other marine animals would also be important for hiring consideration. Even when hiring Aquarists who are familiar with fish and their habits, many aquariums assign new workers to trainee positions for 6 months to a year. They work with experienced persons to learn to recognize signs of disease, behavior characteristics of various species, and other factors critical to the preservation of the animals and the operation of the institution. Some hiring establishments require that Aquarists be certified scuba divers, so that they can participate in the underwater collection of aquatic life.

HELPFUL PERSONAL CHARACTERISTICS

Aquarists should be interested in marine life, and in following the fairly regular schedule of feeding, cleaning, and monitoring necessary to maintain it.

Although taking care of fish, tortoises, porpoises, and other colorful and exotic creatures might sound exciting, most of the work involved is routine, and persons interested in these jobs should be able to adjust to a work schedule that is likely to be the same, day after day.

Aquarists should be alert to recognize changes in appearance or behavior that may indicate the presence of disease. This is especially important because the disease might spread to other creatures in the same tank, causing the decimation of the collection and a possible financial catastrophe for the institution.

PHYSICAL DEMANDS AND ENVIRONMENTAL CONDITIONS

This is medium to heavy work, requiring that the worker be in excellent physical condition. Because many of the tasks may be performed underwater, it is hard to apply the usual standards of weights lifted or moved to evaluate strength requirements. The pressure of water on both the Aquarist and equipment makes even the movement of fairly light objects difficult, and the work can be physically demanding. Aquarists should be able to move about easily underwater, so that physical discomfort will not interfere with performance of duties.

WHERE TO FIND THESE JOBS

Aquarists work at commercial and nonprofit aquariums, operated autonomously or as part of a science center complex, science museum, or zoo. Oceanariums, which specialize in the display, study, and preservation of salt water fish, reptiles, and mammals, are most likely to require that their Aquarists also be scuba divers.

OPPORTUNITIES FOR EMPLOYMENT AND PROMOTION

Because there are fewer than 50 aquariums in the United States, there are never more than a few openings for Aquarists at any given time. Chances for employment in this field are probably better in the large, commercially operated aquariums and marine life-oriented recreational facilities than in aquariums maintained as nonprofit institutions or as divisions of zoos, museums, or science centers. Many of this latter group are operated by cities, and Aquarists are hired through civil service channels. Inquiries about employment should be made at civil service headquarters for the various communities, or at the personnel offices of commercial aquariums and ocean parks.

At establishments employing a number of Aquarists, these workers may advance to supervisory positions. However, there is little possibility of promotion to other jobs without additional education.

ARCHEOLOGICAL ASSISTANT

OCCUPATIONAL STATEMENT

Prepares digs (archeological excavations) and cleans, restores, and preserves archeological specimens and historical artifacts according to accepted chemical and physical techniques, training in archeological science, and instructions of crew leader: Works as part of crew to prepare archeological excavation, according to boundaries indicated by chalk or stakes, using shovel and pickax. Excavates pottery, bones, implements, and other archeological specimens, exercising care to keep specimens intact. Removes soil and dirt from specimens, using scraper and dusting broom. Reports objects found to crew leader, and records date, location, and tentative identification of objects in project logbook. Cleans and repairs or reinforces specimens, such as weapons, mummified remains, and pottery, using handtools and prescribed chemical agents. Restores artifacts by polishing, joining together fragments, or other procedures, using hand and power tools and acid, chemical, or electrolytic corrosion-removal baths. Treats specimens to prevent or minimize deterioration, according to accepted procedures. Prepares detailed drawings of specimens, noting dimensions, material, and position in strata of excavation, for inclusion with records. Prepares reports of activities. May plan and conduct research to improve methods of restoring and preserving specimens.

EDUCATION, TRAINING, AND EXPERIENCE

Jobs as Archeological Assistants are of two types, with slightly different hiring requirements for each. Temporary jobs in this field are available during summer to students who may or may not be working toward bachelor's or advanced degrees in anthropology or a related social science. Hiring for these jobs may be based on scholastic achievement, previous experience with similar projects, evidence of interest on the part of the job applicant, or participation in a government-subsidized job or vocational training program. The Archeological Assistant in these jobs usually does not receive academic credit; the practical experience gained however, is invaluable to budding social scientists.

Permanent positions in this work are open to persons with academic training in anthropology or archeology. Although a degree is preferred, many establishments will hire and train persons without one. In fact, some State museums have participated with high schools in their areas in government-sponsored workstudy programs, through which students earn money and learn the less complex techniques of artifact identification, preservation, and restoration.

Archeological Assistants with advanced training are likely to be assigned more difficult duties from the time of their hiring, but even they are required to work under the close supervision of a staff archeologist, Curator, or other personal in charge of the expedition or the conservation facilities.

HELPFUL PERSONAL CHARACTERISTICS

Persons in this kind of work should have intellectual curiosity, an interest in both science and history, the willingness to do hard physical work, and clerical aptitude.

Summer workers could get by with only the last two characteristics, if they are not interested in this kind of work as a full-time job. Persons desiring a career in this field, however, should have acquired the knowledge to recognize unearthed specimens as belonging to a certain period of civilization, as well as the ability to do the careful manual work needed to join parts of shattered objects, treat them with preservatives, or apply coatings to restore them.

PHYSICAL DEMANDS AND ENVIRONMENTAL CONDITIONS

The physical requirements of this job vary from light to heavy, depending on the emphasis placed on the excavating and restoring tasks of individual positions. In field work, heavy manual labor is required, using shovels, spades, and pickaxes.

Many excavating expeditions take place in the hottest part of the summer, or in parts of the world that are always uncomfortably hot and steamy, or hot and arid. Persons interested in this kind of archeological work should be able to function well in such climates, and also be able to adjust to living for extended periods in tents or trailers, where they may be subject to all of the inconveniences of camping. On-site examination and preservation work is usually done in temporary laboratories set up for the expedition.

For full-time Archeological Assistants, the outdoor excavating period represents a relatively small portion of their activities. Most of the study, classification, and restoration of artifacts is done in the comfortable, climate-controlled surroundings of a laboratory or studio operated by the sponsoring institution.

WHERE TO FIND THESE JOBS

Archeological Assistants work for science museums, national or State parks in areas of archeological significance, some colleges and universities, and certain nonprofit research institutions.

OPPORTUNITIES FOR EMPLOYMENT AND PROMOTION

People interested in summer jobs of this type should apply to the appropriate institution no later than February to find out about openings and hiring requirements. Openings for full-time positions are often filled by persons with vacation experience with the same establishment. The institutions most likely to hire persons for these jobs are located in areas where archeological studies are made—primarily the Southwest and Mountain States—or in large metropolitan centers with several museums and universities cooperating in carrying out such projects.

Opportunities for employment vary from place to place, and depend largely on funds available for research.

There is no automatic advancement assured for workers in these jobs. Frequently, recent graduates with degrees in anthropology or archeology may find work as assistants to Curators or faculty members, advancing to higher positions when the incumbents leave. However, there are very few establishments where a definable career ladder exists.

ARCHIVIST

OCCUPATIONAL STATEMENT

Appraises and edits permanent records and historically valuable documents, participates in research activities based on archival materials, and directs safekeeping of archival documents and materials: Analyzes documents, such as government records, minutes of corporate board meetings, letters from famous persons, and charters of nonprofit organizations; ascertains date of writing, author, or original recipient of letter to appraise value to posterity or to the employing organization. Directs activities of workers engaged in cataloging and safekeeping of valuable materials and directs disposition of worthless materials. Prepares or directs preparation of document descriptions and reference aids for use of archives, such as accession lists, indexes, guides, bibliographies, abstracts, and microfilmed copies of documents. Directs filing and crossindexing of selected documents in alphabetical and chronological order. Advises government agencies, scholars, journalists, and others conducting research by supplying available materials and information according to familiarity with archives and with political, economic, military, and social history of period. Requests or recommends pertinent materials available in libraries, private collections, or other archives. Selects and edits documents for publication and display, according to knowledge of subject, literary or journalistic expression, and techniques for presentation and display. May be designated according to subject matter specialty as Archivist, economic history Archivist, political history Archivist, military history or according to nature of employing institution as Archivist, nonprofit foundation. In smaller organizations, may direct activities of libraries.

EDUCATION, TRAINING AND EXPERIENCE

The work of Archivists is quite similar to that of librarians, and vocational preparation for archival work should include some library courses. However, since Archivists are involved with manuscripts, documents, and other items of historical significance, they should also have academic training in history in order to identify, describe, and classify materials in the collection. In large institutions, archival work may be done by a number of persons, each of whom cares for historic materials related to a specific period of time, or particular area (for example, Civil War history, or Middle European history). For jobs such as these, employers usually require appropriate academic specialization in addition to other training. Similarly, Archivists may be in charge of single segments of collections (for example, photographs, or architectural drawings and building plans), and be required to have the technical knowledge to classify these materials. Most Archivists have bachelor of arts degrees in history and acquire technical expertise by participating in one or more of the archival graduate programs, workshops, and seminars offered by a number of universities. These provide training in classification methods, preservation and storage techniques, and data retrieval systems. In some large institutions, archival records may be computerized, requiring that Archivists also be trained in computer input, storage, and retrieval methods.

Internships, offered to upperclassmen or graduate students by museums or historical associations, provide paid, learning-while working experience to many persons who wish to become Archivists These may or may not lead to permanent jobs with the same institution, but all enhance employment opportunities.

Persons with bachelor of art degrees in history and an interest in archival work may be hired as assistants to Archivists and be given on-the-job training to prepare them for professional duties.

HELPFUL PERSONAL CHARACTERISTICS

Although the Occupational Statement for this job may imply that all Archivists head staffs of workers who do the major cataloging and description writing of materials, this is not the case. In most institutions, the administrative and supervisory duties of Archivists are minimal, and do not require the ability to plan or oversee the operation of a large department.

Archivists often work alone, except for occasional contacts with other persons who use the institution materials for research. They should be able to adjust to the semi-isolation of their work quarters, and to devote total concentration to the study and classification of materials.

The successful Archivist has an inquiring mind, a retentive memory, and the ability to read and comprehend both handwritten and printed materials quickly and selectively, in order to extract pertinent information from them. Skill in organizing this information and writing concise and clear descriptions of materials for catalogs and file cards is also important.

Organizational and clerical aptitudes are needed to maintain storage and retrieval facilities in such a way that both institution personnel and visiting researchers can locate materials easily.

People doing archival work should feel comfortable working by themselves. Compulsive talkers would never be happy in this kind of work. Compulsive scholars might find that it was truly designed with them in mind.

PHYSICAL DEMANDS AND ENVIRONMENTAL CONDITIONS

This is sedentary work, making few physical demands on the worker. Because of the frequent examination of documents and other materials, as well as the reading requirements of the job, good eyesight is extremely important. The work is usually performed in a quiet, library-like atmosphere.

WHERE TO FIND THESE JOBS

Archivists work in history, museum field, they may also be ethnic, and specialty museums; facilities maintained and operated by State, county, and local historical societies; and certain federally owned institutions, monuments, or other installations. Outside of the museum field, they may also be employed by libraries, universities, nonprofit organizations, and certain business or industrial establishments.

OPPORTUNITIES FOR EMPLOYMENT AND PROMOTION

Archives work is one of the fastest growing segments of the history profession, and offers numerous opportunities for employment. Persons with the appropriate academic background, plus the necessary temperament, should have little trouble finding this kind of work. A number of Federal jobs are found at such institutions as the National Archives, Library of Congress, and other installations throughout the country. State governments, as well as historical associations, also employ Archivists. The most practical way of locating potential job opportunities is to contact the public or private agencies involved to find out what qualifications they look for in applicants, and what their hiring procedures—civil service registers, job announcements, acceptance of resumes—are, and then follow through according to the rules.

Most jobs in this field are full time; however, a number of county or local historical societies look for qualified persons to fill part-time archival positions.

Chances for advancement are limited according to the size of the hiring institution, as well as the number of positions in the department. Generally, there is little possibility of promotion except in government jobs or those with extremely large museums or historical societies.

ART CONSERVATOR

OCCUPATIONAL STATEMENT

Coordinates activities of subordinates engaged in examination, repair, and conservation of art objects, such as paintings, statuary, tapestries, or china, or historically significant items such as documents, furnishings, ethnological materials, or textiles: Examines and tests properties of objects to determine condition, need for repair, methods of preservation or restoration, and authenticity, using X-rays, radiographs, microscopes, laser beams, heating devices, and physical and chemical testing equipment and solutions. Assigns repair or restoration duties to subordinates, according to type and composition of objects and expertise of workers. Oversees or participates in restoration projects. Directs or advises Curators and technical staff on handling, mounting, care, packing, shipping, and storing of objects. Advises building maintenance personnel on proper temperature, humidity, and light levels for gallery and storage areas to prevent deterioration or damage to objects. Estimates cost of restoration work. May examine objects prior to shipment from museum to determine condition and value, to establish insurance requirements in transit. May examine and treat objects belonging to other institutions.

EDUCATION, TRAINING, AND EXPERIENCE

Conservators must have completed lengthy formal education and training, and have had extensive work experience as acknowledged experts in the restoration and conservation of such objects or materials as paintings, sculpture, china, paper, or textiles.

Undergraduate work would have included chemistry, physics, and other sciences, as well as courses in the standard curriculum for a bachelor's degree in art history, art, museology, or a related field.

Graduate work would have been done at one of the few institutions in the United States where conservation training is available, among them, Oberlin College in Ohio, New York University in New York City, and the Winterthur Museum in Delaware.

At these or other institutions, the aspiring conservator would have learned the techniques needed to restore, repair, and preserve a variety of objects fashioned from many materials. During this training period, he or she would probably choose one or more of these specialties for intensive study, and receive a graduate degree or certificate with the notation of proficiency in that particular field.

After completing graduate training, would-be conservators usually work as Museum Interns in the conservation laboratories of museums, nonprofit organizations, or commercial enterprises. During the internships, they have the opportunity of earning and learning, under the supervision of an experienced conservator or restoration specialist. Full-time employment follows, as a specialist skilled in the techniques of preserving or restoring works of art, documents, textiles, or other items.

Employment in a special field should be accompanied by the continued study of the appropriate techniques for treating other objects. The combination of the intensive practice of preservative and restorative methods in one field, plus extensive knowledge of this sort of work in other fields, provides the background necessary for hiring consideration for jobs as conservator.

HELPFUL PERSONAL CHARACTERISTICS

Conservators must have the basic intelligence and verbal and mathematical aptitudes to learn and apply a wide variety of scientific and artistic techniques. They also need manual and finger dexterity, eye-hand coordination, visual acuity, and color perception, to repair or restore works of art and other objects, demonstrate techniques to subordinates, and evaluate their work.

Conservators must be perfectionists, both in performing their own work, and judging the work of others. They must be able to make decisions based on both measurable and sensory factors, to determine the appropriate methods for restoring objects, and to evaluate the results of restorations.

They should be articulate, not only to discuss problems and explain methods of conservation and restoration, but also to compose reports and articles.

Administrative and clerical abilities are needed to organize and direct the operation of the conservation facility.

PHYSICAL DEMANDS AND ENVIRONMENTAL CONDITIONS

The conservator's work is usually not physically demanding, although certain assignments involving the restoration of exceptionally large pieces—tapestries or statuary, for example—may require working on scaffolding, and reaching, bending, stooping, and balancing. Treatment of objects is done in a laboratory or studio; administrative duties may be performed in an office. Conservators, especially those employed by the Federal Government, may travel frequently, to examine, suggest restoration methods for, or treat various objects displayed at other establishments.

WHERE TO FIND THESE JOBS

Large art and multi-discipline museums employ conservators, as do some of the larger restored communities and estates. Federally employed conservators may work at the National Park Service Museum Service Center, at Harpers Ferry, W.Va., the Smithsonian Institution in Washington, D.C., and several other sites. Others work for or operate conservation laboratories maintained by groups of museums in a particular area or with a common specialty, or at commercial laboratories which provide conservation or restoration advice and services.

OPPORTUNITIES FOR EMPLOYMENT AND PROMOTION

The vocational preparation for these jobs is so lengthy and intellectually demanding that relatively few persons have completed it. There is a constant demand for the services of well-qualified Art Conservators, and for those who have the perseverance and ability to complete the training, employment opportunities are many. Because this is the top job in its field, there is little opportunity for advancement except by moving to a more prestigious or better paying position with another institution.

AUDIOVISUAL TECHNICIAN

OCCUPATIONAL STATEMENT

Operates motion picture or slide projectors, tape or record players, or other audiovisual equipment to provide or complement educational or public service programs offered by museum, zoo, or similar institution: Operates motion picture projecting equipment to show films in auditorium or lecture hall for entertainment or enlightenment of institution visitors. Operates film, slide, video, audiotape, or turntable equipment to project or produce still or moving pictures, background music, oral commentary, or sound effects, to illustrate, clarify, or enhance impact of address, lecture, or other presentation by Teacher or other person. Coordinates equipment operation with material presented according to notations in script, or instructions of speaker. Maintains equipment in working order. Makes minor adjustments and repairs of equipment, and notifies maintenance personnel when correction of major malfunctions is required. May also position, install, and connect microphones, amplifiers, banks of lights, and other equipment.

EDUCATION, TRAINING, AND EXPERIENCE

Audiovisual Technicians should know how to operate and make minor repairs on projectors and other audiovisual equipment. This knowledge may have been acquired through work experience or vocational training in high school, trade school, or junior college. There are no set educational requirements for such jobs.

HELPFUL PERSONAL CHARACTERISTICS

Persons in these jobs should have good manual and finger dexterity, to operate, control, and adjust equipment. They should be able to concentrate totally on the job, in order to start and stop equipment precisely, so that the appropriate images and sounds are seen and heard on schedule.

PHYSICAL DEMANDS AND ENVIRONMENTAL CONDITIONS

This is usually light work, performed in pleasant indoor surroundings. Good eyesight is needed to follow written cues and control equipment when work is being done in projection booths or in dimly lit auditoriums. In locations where equipment is not stationary and must be moved and set up before every use, physical strength may be needed to lift equipment onto and off of handtrucks, and to move such equipment as amplifiers and light banks into proper positions.

WHERE TO FIND THESE JOBS

Audiovisual Technicians work at art, science, and history museums, in planetariums, and in other institutions that offer extensive education and public service programs. They also may work in facilities operated by the National Park Service, and at certain State parks and monuments.

OPPORTUNITIES FOR EMPLOYMENT AND PROMOTION

Just as with other jobs in the educational or public service category, the job of Audiovisual Technician is most likely to be found in large city institutions. In museums in smaller communities or rural areas, the tasks of this worker would most likely be performed by a Teacher or some other institution employee; there is little likelihood that the number of programs presented would be large enough to warrant hiring a full-time Audiovisual Technician. However, as the accent on education in these institutions continues to grow, smaller establishments may have openings for workers such as these. Part-time employment in this field is nearly always available to persons with the needed skills and experience. Motion-picture projectionists, or persons who showed slides or ran projectors while in school, would receive first consideration for such part-time openings. Inquiry about such jobs in National or State park systems should be made at the facility involved. The Park Superintendent should have information about openings, and the appropriate civil service procedures to be followed for hiring consideration.

Except in very large institutions, there is little chance of advancement from this job to others in the establishment.

COMMISSARY ASSISTANT

OCCUPATIONAL STATEMENT

Stores, prepares, and delivers foods for zoo or aquarium animals: Unloads meats, produce, fodder, and other food items from delivery vehicle, using handtruck to move items into commissary for inspection by supervisor. Sorts and stores items on shelves, in bins, or refrigerated storage room. Assembled food items needed for diet of various animals, as directed by supervisor. Measures, weighs, or counts items to obtain amount of food specified for various diet plans Bundles fodder to prepare for conveyance to animal quarters. Washes product and cuts defects from items. Sorts assembled items into groups according to animal quarters for which they are intended. Loads items into truck, drives truck to various animal quarters, and assists keepers in carrying food to preparation areas. When keepers come to commissary to pick up food for charges, assists in selecting and loading food into truck or cart.

EDUCATION TRAINING, AND EXPERIENCE

There are no set hiring requirements for this job, other than the ability to drive. High school graduates are preferred, but persons with less formal education are often considered. No previous experience is needed. In large zoos, a week or so of on-the-job training is given to new assistants by commissary supervisors, to help them become familiar with locations of all animal quarters and with the basic types of diet required by different species of animals. In smaller zoos, such training might be given by a consulting veterinarian, head keeper, or other staff member in charge of planning appropriate diets.

HELPFUL PERSONAL CHARACTERISTICS

Commissary Assistants should be willing to follow fairly routine work patterns, doing the same thing day after day to load, store, and prepare animal foods. They should be able to follow directions for properly storing various kinds of food, and be willing to exercise care in weighing, measuring, and mixing foods according to specifications.

PHYSICAL DEMANDS AND ENVIRONMENTAL CONDITIONS

This is active work, requiring both physical strength and agility to unload, carry, and store bales of straw or hay or cartons of raw meat or produce weighing 50 pounds or more. Although hand trucks are used to move the heaviest items, the worker needs strength, especially in arms and shoulders, to lift them on to and off of trucks or carts. Average manual dexterity is needed to sort, wash, and cut defects from foods. Most of the work is done in the warehouse atmosphere of the zoo commissary, although unloading and delivery of foods must be done outdoors at least once a day in all kinds of weather.

WHERE TO FIND THESE JOBS

Most large and medium-sized zoos and aquariums employ workers in this position. In the smallest zoos, all commissary duties—ordering, storing, and preparation of provision—are frequently performed by one person, who may be assisted by keepers.

OPPORTUNITIES FOR EMPLOYMENT AND PROMOTION

About half of the country's 240 zoos and aquariums hire their workers from municipal civil service lists; the others hire at establishment offices. Because not all zoos have this position available, there are fewer opportunities than for other jobs such as keeper. Government employment and training programs like CETA often subsidize jobs such as this one, thereby fulfilling the dual purpose of helping zoos operate more efficiently and providing meaningful work for people who need it. Commissary Assistants who have a good math background or aptitude, plus the ability to deal with representatives of businesses that sell the various kinds of animal food, can advance to the position of commissary manager or zoo purchasing agent.

CRAFT CENTER DIRECTOR

OCCUPATIONAL STATEMENT

Plans, organizes, and directs activities of handcraft center operated by folk or history museum, historic or ethnic area or community, or historic or regional theme park: Consults with administrative personnel to plan center activities, such as craft classes, exhibits, and other projects conducted in cooperation with sponsoring institution. Orders supplies needed for basketry, leatherwork, candlemaking, macrame, tole painting, beadwork, or other crafts compatible with institution's theme. Plans and writes publicity material for craft classes and supervises instructors engaged to conduct classes. Plans and supervises presentation of craft shows and exhibits, arranging for crafters specializing in handiwork of various kinds to participate, and overseeing installation of exhibit booths, distribution of publicity materials, and scheduling of craft demonstrations. Maintains inventory, personnel, and accounting records for craft center. When center's activities include sale of craft items, arranges for consignment of articles made by craft workers, sets prices of articles, supervises sales personnel, and maintains records of operation. Reports operational activities to institution's administrative staff or governing body and works with staff to plan and implement changes in operation or facilities. May teach one or more craft courses. May organize traveling shows of craft work. May supervise Craft Demonstrators engaged in demonstrating crafts in museum, community, or park exhibit area.

EDUCATION, TRAINING, AND EXPERIENCE

This job requires a combination of training and experience that couples familiarity with a number of crafts, and probably skill in one or more of them, with administrative or high-level clerical work background. Although the accent might be on one or another kind of training and experience, some success in both creative and business fields is required. Thus, experience in making pottery, required either through formal instruction or as a self-taught hobby, plus experience managing a gift shop might be an acceptable background for this kind of work; so would a degree in business administration and some experience in teaching ceramics on a part-time basis; or volunteer work stocking and keeping records of a museum gift shop with skill in doing macrame and painting designs on china. Individual establishment hiring requirements may vary, with primary emphasis placed on either the craft or the business background, but all stress the need for both kinds of experience or training.

HELPFUL PERSONAL CHARACTERISTICS

Craft Center Directors should be imaginative, well organized, able to plan and follow through on complete projects, and capable of keeping accurate records. Jobs such as these include such a variety of tasks that you must be able to adapt quickly and completely from one to another set of duties; for instance, from teaching and demonstrating methods of making beaded belts, to writing publicity material for craft shows, to using an adding machine to total sales of the craft center shop. Imagination is needed to devise innovative display and publicity techniques. The ability to speak well and to get along well with people at all levels— administrative staff, fellow workers, and the general public—is also important. Although the job does not require physical strength in the usual sense, it does call for constant energy and enthusiasm to carry out all of the duties successfully.

PHYSICAL DEMANDS AND ENVIRONMENTAL CONDITIONS

This is usually active work, involving moving around the craft center, demonstrating crafts, storing or handling craft supplies, and traveling in the area to visit other craft workers, supervise the installation of display facilities, and attend meetings and seminars. Although the job is primarily administrative, craft teaching and demonstration require skillful use of tools or equipment. In most places, the work is done in comfortable studio-like quarters on the museum premises. Some overnight traveling may be required to supervise or participate in craft shows or fairs.

WHERE TO FIND THESE JOBS

This is a relatively new job, emerging as the result both of the popularity of handicrafts as hobbies and of the public interest in traditional customs and various ethnic practices. Craft Center Directors may work for history museums or folk museums, or for historic or ethnic areas, either restored or simulated, which concentrate on particular kinds of handmade objects. Some of these have separate buildings on the institution's grounds, while others are located in the section of the museum devoted to educational activities. Theme parks, which may be built around pioneer, American Indian, or early American life, often have craft centers that serve area residents and tourists alike.

OPPORTUNITIES FOR EMPLOYMENT AND PROMOTION

Employment opportunities for this kind of work have been improving since the bicentennial, when many institutions expanded their programs to include this type of community project. Many people get into this work after having done craft instruction or demonstration in the community. Institutions may consider initiating such a project if they are approached by people with the needed craft-and-business background, especially if they can be convinced that class fees and/or shop sales would provide revenue. This kind of work affords a good opportunity for job development for enterprising people. There would, however, be little opportunity to advance to other jobs, except with a large establishment maintaining several craft centers at different locations.

CRAFT DEMONSTRATOR

OCCUPATIONAL STATEMENT

Demonstrates and explains techniques and purpose of handicraft, or other activity such as candle dipping, horseshoeing, or soapmaking, as part of display in history or folk museum, or restored or refurbished farm, village, or neighborhood: Studies historical and technical literature to acquire information about time period and lifestyle depicted in display and craft techniques associated with that time and area, to devise plan for authentic presentation of craft. Work with research personnel to draft outline of talk to acquaint visitors with customs and crafts associated with folklife depicted in display. Practices techniques involved in handicraft to assure accurate and skillful demonstration. Molds candles, shoes horses, operates looms, or engages in other craft or activity, working in appropriate period setting, to demonstrate craft to visitors. Explains techniques of craft, and points out relationship of craft to lifestyle depicted to assist visitors to comprehend traditional techniques of work and play peculiar to time and areas. Answers visitors' questions or refers visitors to other sources for information. May portray role of actual person or fictitious character living in time and area depicted, presenting explanation in first person. May participate in dramatic productions to interpret traditional lifestyle or historical events associated with display or restored area.

EDUCATION, TRAINING, AND EXPERIENCE

There are no set educational requirements for this kind of work, although high school graduation is usually needed. Some experience in public contact work or in amateur or professional theatrics is helpful. Familiarity with the craft(s) to be demonstrated is needed, whether acquired through practicing a hobby or by formal training. In a few establishments, training in some of the less complex crafts and activities, such as soapmaking or operation of a simple gristmill, is given to inexperienced workers after hiring. All Craft Demonstrators are given formal or informal training to make them familiar with facts about the lifestyle depicted in the work setting. They may then describe these while demonstrating their crafts and also be prepared to answer visitors' questions.

HELPFUL PERSONAL CHARACTERISTICS

Craft Demonstrators should be interested both in working with their hands and in dealing with the public. They need at least average manual and finger dexterity to demonstrate the craft work or other activity. In some establishments, the items produced by craft workers are sold to visitors, and the workmanship of these articles must be more professional than of those where the craft is demonstrated by items not even completed. Craft Demonstrators should be poised and able to speak easily to the public. In situations where they act out roles, either alone or as members of a cast, they should have some acting ability (plus a good memory for their lines) in order to make their performances believable and to contribute to the institution's total effect.

PHYSICAL DEMANDS AND ENVIRONMENTAL CONDITIONS

These vary according to the craft demonstrated and the work setting. All positions require the almost constant use of the hands, plus constant speaking. However, the assignment of showing how the village blacksmith used to shape horseshoes requires much more physical strength and activity than that of demonstrating how sunbonnets were sewn by hand: the demonstrator who works in the air-conditioned reproduction of a 19th-century kitchen will be much more comfortable than the one who works outdoors, stacking hay in the simulated pasture of a 19th-century farm.

WHERE TO FIND THESE JOBS

Craft Demonstrators work in history, industrial, and folklife museums, as well as in restored or simulated villages, farms, or neighborhoods that depict the way things were at a specific time and place. They are also employed at certain State and national parks which have historic or ethnic themes. People who are primarily craft workers may also find this kind of work in commercially operated theme parks.

OPPORTUNITIES FOR EMPLOYMENT AND PROMOTION

This job is relatively new to the museum scene, having come into existence during the 1960s, when "living museums," "interpretation" in the park systems, and public interest in both nostalgia and environmental preservation became important parts of the American culture. There are already a number of institutions that employ Craft Demonstrators, and there are likely to be more in years to come. Opportunities for part-time or seasonal work are especially good because so many employing institutions feature outdoor facilities. Persons skilled in a craft and interested in this kind of work should contact the museum or other facilities, during the off-season (January or February), to find out what hiring requirements are. For jobs in State and national parks, taking the appropriate civil service examination may be the first step.

Without further education or training, there is little chance for advancement from this job except in a few very large community restoration projects.

CURATOR

OCCUPATIONAL STATEMENT

Provides professional care for objects in collection, plans and conducts research, participates in planning and implementation of special projects, and oversees activities of workers in museum, zoo, or other institution: Works with administrators to acquire articles or specimens for collection through purchase, gifts, field work, or transfer from other institution. Studies, examines, tests acquisitions to determine or authenticate origin, composition, history, and current value, utilizing appropriate techniques, and basing evaluation on knowledge of specialized area of science, art, or history to which items relate. Assigns code numbers to items and records descriptive information to assist registrar, or maintain institution's registration files, and to provide resource material for planning exhibit, education, publication, and research activities. Consults with other staff members to determine factors critical to preservation of collection; institutes appropriate procedures, such as control of temperature, humidity, exposure to light, and protection from damage by insects, fungus, or bacteria to preserve items in storage or exhibit areas. Inspects collection items regularly and confers with conservation personnel to determine and implement activities to restore or repair damaged or deteriorated items. Works with other staff members to plan and organize educational, public service, special exhibit, and other projects. Plans, executes, or participates in research or field studies, and publishes articles or lectures on results. Represents institution at conferences and seminars. Directs and coordinates activities of workers, graduate students, and Museum Interns assigned to department, and assists students in planning and carrying out projects for academic credit. May teach classes for institution or college. May prepare proposals for financial support by outside agencies and be responsible for administration of grant funds. In small institutions, may also perform duties of Director.

EDUCATION, TRAINING, AND EXPERIENCE

Hiring requirements for Curators vary, according to both the size and type of the employing establishment. Minimum educational requirement in almost all places would be graduation from college, with a major in a field compatible with the institution's theme or, when responsibility for only a portion of a collection is involved, academic specialization in the appropriate field. The minimum work experience requirement would be a year or two as assistant or associate curator in the same or a similar establishment, several years as a Research Associate or Museum Intern, or several years in a university teaching or research position involved with the same subject matter as the curatorial opening. Most medium to large museums require that Curators have at least a master's degree or, preferably, a doctorate in their field of specialization, plus training and work experience that provided both extensive, broad knowledge of a particular discipline and intensive, concentrated knowledge of a specialization within that discipline. Consideration is also given to applicants' publication records, research objectives, and professional recommendations. In science-oriented establishments, such as zoos, botanical gardens, and natural history museums, participation in field trips, successful building of collections of specimens, and service as officers of scientific societies also add to the qualifications. Art museums look for Curators with firsthand familiarity with panicular types of art work, for example, early oriental porcelains or primitive African art, in-depth knowledge of methods of maintaining and restoring art works, and established reputations as experts in their fields.

A few establishments have less demanding requirements: zoos, in particular, may hire Curators with less academic background if they are thoroughly versed and highly experienced in animal care techniques. Small museums of all kinds (those employing fewer than 20 or so people) are often willing to hire Curators with less academically impressive credentials. However, curatorial work is primarily scholar oriented, with or without extensive academic background, and employing institutions of all types and sizes evaluate the formal education and scholarly achievements of applicants.

PHYSICAL DEMANDS

This is generally light work, performed in pleasant indoor offices or laboratories. A notable exception to this is found in curatorial positions involving extensive field trips or expeditions to collect or study specimens.

HELPFUL PERSONAL CHARACTERISTICS

People wishing to become Curators should have intellectual curiosity, interest in research, the ability to concentrate, and an orderly, organized mind, all qualities needed to succeed academically and to perform the duties associated with this kind of work. Because preparation of papers and delivery of lectures is also part of most jobs, would-be Curators should also be able to express themselves well, both orally and in writing. An absorbing interest in the chosen field, whether archeology, European history, or ichthyology, is a definite requirement, along with the other qualities that each special interest demands. The ability to think creatively is also helpful in planning and conducting research and interpreting the results in a way that expresses new ideas or adds to the fundamental knowledge of a particular field. Curators who also function as Directors should have supervisory ability and business aptitudes in addition to their other qualities.

WHERE TO FIND THESE JOBS

Curators work in large and small museums of all kinds; in zoos, botanical gardens, arboretums, and herbariums; in State and national parks which have collections of items of historical, scientific, or natural significance; and in historic homes, shrines, and other noteworthy buildings.

OPPORTUNITIES FOR EMPLOYMENT AND PROMOTION

These vary from time to time and place to place. If museums and other institutions continue to receive more public money, opportunities for college-trained people with degrees in science, art, or history should increase. CETA is now funding some curatorial positions; in addition, others are open to persons who do not qualify for CETA-related job placement. Curators can go on to become Directors or, in very large, departmentalized museums, can become chief curators, exercising general supervision over a number of other Curators.

DEVELOPMENT DIRECTOR

OCCUPATIONAL STATEMENT

Plans, organizes, directs, and coordinates ongoing and special project funding programs for museum, zoo, or similar institution: Confers with administrative personnel and representatives of institution's governing body to determine needs for general operations and for such special projects as expansion of physical facilities or acquisition of particular works of art. Prepares statement of planned activities and enlists support for various phases of plan from members of institution staff and volunteer organizations. Develops public relations materials to enhance institution's image and promote fund-raising projects. Identifies potential contributors to special project funds and supporters of institution's ongoing operations through examination of past records, individual and corporate contacts, and knowledge of community. Plans and coordinates fund drives for special projects, assigning responsibilities for personal solicitations to members of staff, volunteer organizations, and governing body, according to individuals' special interests or capabilities, and organizing direct mail campaign to reach other potential contributors. Plans and supervises other benefit events, such as banquets, balls, or auctions. Establishes ongoing support for institution by organizing solicitation drive for pledges of funds from individuals, corporations, and foundations. Informs potential contributors of special needs of institution and encourages individuals, corporations, and foundations to establish, or contribute to, special funds through endowments, trusts, donations of gifts-in-kind, or bequests; confers with attorneys to establish methods of transferring funds to benefit both donors and institution. Identifies other sources of funding for research, community service, or other projects by researching public and private grant agencies and foundations. Writes and submits proposals for grants to agencies and foundations, obtaining information about proposals from personnel requesting grants, and following established format and procedures. Supervises and coordinates activities of workers engaged in maintaining records of all contributors and grants, and preparing letters of appreciation to be sent to contributors.

EDUCATION, TRAINING, AND EXPERIENCE

Development Directors should have bachelor's degrees in business administration or a similar field, with specialization in public relations, marketing, or financial management. Training or work experience in grants work (preparing and submitting applications and proposals for financial grants, on behalf of nonprofit institutions or non-Federal Government agencies) is a frequent requirement. Although some institutions will hire recent graduates for these jobs, most require that applicants have 2 or more years of experience in public relations or other public contact work. Experience with other nonprofit institutions, or in any position whose duties involved dealing with the area's financial or cultural community, is especially desirable.

HELPFUL PERSONAL CHARACTERISTICS

Development Directors should enjoy working with other people, be able to organize their thoughts to make plans and follow through on them, and have good oral and written communications skills. In addition, they must be able to generate enthusiasm for the employing institution and its projects, and to maintain this enthusiasm and transmit it to potential contributors, other staff members, and volunteers. Imagination and a sense of showmanship are helpful in devising fund-raising activities and preparing publicity for them, but these should be tempered by the practicality of carrying out the activities and evaluating their relevance to the aims and image of the institution. Business sense is needed to understand and explain the various kinds of financial support that the institution should encourage and to draft grant proposals according to established language and procedural rules.

PHYSICAL DEMANDS AND ENVIRONMENTAL CONDITIONS

The Development Director should have both mental and physical stamina to maintain constant enthusiasm for the job and to remain alert, knowledgeable, and interested in the comments and questions of institution and governing body staff members and of potential contributors. Because there are frequent evening meetings and social functions associated with the job, as well as occasional out-of-town commitments, the Development Director does not work the standard 8-hour day. People interested in this kind of work should realize that it can be mentally and physically demanding and that they may have to curtail some of their personal social and recreational activities to fulfill their professional obligations.

WHERE TO FIND THESE JOBS

The work performed by Development Directors goes on at virtually all museums and similar institutions, except those that are totally funded by a government or private agency and are forbidden to accept other financial support. In many institutions, however, fund-raising may be the responsibility of the Director, the comptroller, other financial officer, or other administrative personnel; in some of the smallest establishments, this function may belong solely to the volunteer groups associated with them.

OPPORTUNITIES FOR EMPLOYMENT AND PROMOTION

More and more museums, large and small and of every type, are hiring Development Directors as full-time workers. With the expected continued support of museum-related institutions by both public and private agencies and foundations, the need for qualified people to write and submit proposals for grants will steadily increase. Most institutions need more money in order to keep up with the public demands for their services; most are finding that assigning the responsibility for all fund-developing functions to a single person, rather than to various staff members, is the most efficient way of getting the job done.

DIRECTOR

OCCUPATIONAL STATEMENT

Administers affairs of museum, zoo, or similar establishment: Confers with institution's board of directors to formulate policies and plan overall operations. Directs acquisitional, education, research, public service, and development activities of institution, consulting with curatorial, administrative, and maintenance staff members to implement policies and initiate programs, and exercising broad supervision over operations. Works with members of curatorial and administrative staffs to acquire additions to collections. Works with administrative staff members to determine budget requirements, plan fund-raising drives, prepare applications for grants from government agencies or private foundations, and solicit financial support for institution. Establishes and maintains contact with administrators of other institutions to exchange information concerning operations and plan, coordinate, or consolidate community service and education programs. Maintains contact with members of institution's governing body and support organizations, to discuss operations, suggest changes in policies, and solicit assistance of members in carrying out institution programs. Represents institution at professional and civic social events, conventions, and other gatherings, to strengthen relationships with cultural and civic leaders, present lectures or participate in seminars, or explain institution's functions and seek financial support for projects. Reviews materials prepared by staff members, such as articles for journals, requests for grants, and reports on institution programs, and approves materials or suggests changes. May instruct classes in institution's education program or be guest lecturer at university. May write articles for technical journals or other publications. May also perform duties of Curator, exercising more direct supervision of care and use of collection objects. May be designated according to type of institution as museum director. Planetarium director, zoo director, botanical garden director, historical society director.

EDUCATION, TRAINING, AND EXPERIENCE

Directors of museums, zoos, and similar institutions are usually selected because they can lend a measure of prestige to the organization, in addition to having a qualifying background of education and work experience.

The usual educational requirements include an advanced degree in an appropriate field (for example, anthropology or archeology for science museums; astronomy for planetariums; history, art, botany, or zoology for institutions devoted to these fields), plus courses in business administration, public relations, accounting, and museology.

Desirable work experience includes holding lesser administrative posts in the same or similar institution, administrative jobs with other nonprofit, community-oriented organizations, mid- to high-level administrative positions with colleges or universities. Many establishments stress experience in grant proposal writing and familiarity with funding agencies as requirements for hiring consideration. Some also look for Directors who have reputations as scholars in their fields.

In most institutions of this kind, Directors are primarily administrators, and have little need for advanced technical knowledge of the collections because Curators are charged with the care and study of collection objects. However, some establishments—especially history and specialty museums—require Directors to double as Curators, making experience and training in the appropriate field quite important.

HELPFUL PERSONAL CHARACTERISTICS

Because the duties of Directors are so varied, requiring them to function from time to time as administrators, scholars, sales people, or social Directors, they need a variety of personal qualities to perform well in all of these roles.

Since virtually all Directors have had previous experience in administrative jobs, they should already have shown that they work well with people and that they are able to organize information and to schedule their time sensibly.

They should be articulate, poised, and self-assured to feel comfortable when speaking to the community and professional groups, working with the institution's governing body and volunteer organizations, and representing the institution at conferences and workshops.

John Walker, former director of the National Gallery of Art, stated, "Operating a museum was like running any other enterprise in that organization and common sense were basic." He went on to say that in directing a museum, "the added requirements were taste and scholarship."

Different institutions require varying responsibilities on the part of Directors and, therefore, varying personal strengths. Directors of art museums often play major roles in acquiring paintings and other works of art for the collection. They would definitely need the "taste and scholarship" Mr. Walker mentions. Directors of large, multi-discipline museums might spend the greatest portion of their time conferring with other staff members and representatives of other institutions, volunteer organizations, and the institution's governing body. For their positions, organization and common sense would be primary requirements.

The duties performed by each individual Director may require

32

different sets of personal characteristics, and must be examined on an individual basis.

PHYSICAL DEMANDS AND ENVIRONMENTAL CONDITIONS

This is light work which makes no unusual physical demands on the workers. Directors don't always work the standard 8-hour day, because the social and community obligations that are part of the job often include attendance at banquets and other evening functions. Directors of some institutions may spend a good deal of time away from their home base, attending workshops or seminars, or leading or participating in field trips or collecting expeditions.

WHERE TO FIND THESE JOBS

Every museum, zoo, historical society, botanical garden, and similar institution has a Director. State and national parks have Superintendents (whose responsibilities are the same as those of Directors). These jobs are located in urban, suburban, and rural areas all across the country.

OPPORTUNITIES FOR EMPLOYMENT AND ADVANCEMENT

There is a fair amount of turnover in these positions, but, since they are available only to persons who have substantial experience in administrative work, employment opportunities for less experienced workers are not affected. New museums open at the rate of four or five each year, and as persons are named as Directors by these institutions, there are likely to be openings for the positions vacated.

As these are the top jobs in this field, there is no opportunity for advancement within the same institution. However, there is a good deal of job mobility in this kind of work, and Directors of small institutions are frequently given serious consideration for directorial openings in larger ones.

DIRECTOR, ARTS-AND-HUMANITIES COUNCIL

OCCUPATIONAL STATEMENT

Administers program to promote visual and performing arts and humanities: Plans, organizes, and executes creative arts program under authority of governing board. Negotiates contracts and agreements with Federal and State agencies and other cultural organizations for funding and implementation of programs. Establishes statewide councils and provides guidance in obtaining grants, initiating local projects, and disseminating cultural information. Exchanges ideas through seminars, conferences, and other forums and media to accomplish program objectives.

EDUCATION, TRAINING, AND EXPERIENCE

Most of these jobs are with agencies of the various States, and hiring requirements may vary from State to State. All require applicants to have administrative experience in a museum or similar nonprofit organization, familiarity with funding programs and grant application preparation, and knowledge of public relations methods. Most require college graduation, but are not specific as to the discipline. Liberal arts or business administration backgrounds would seem to provide applicants with the most appropriate training; but, because substantial work experience in the administration of a nonprofit organization is the primary requirement, other academic preparation would surely be acceptable.

HELPFUL PERSONAL CHARACTERISTICS

Directors of councils such as these should be articulate, well organized, knowledgeable, and business oriented. They should have done well in school in both English and math classes, and be able to get along well with people from all walks of life.

These characteristics would all apply to administrative jobs in business and industry; to a large extent, this work involves "running a business." In addition to the qualities mentioned above, however, these workers also need an interest in and knowledge of the arts, both visual and performing, and the ability to sustain energy and enthusiasm in order to promote the use and expansion of cultural facilities in the area and throughout the country.

Directors, Arts-and-Humanities, are often thought of as personifying the organizations they head, so people who seek these positions should be aware of the fact that they must be constantly alert, always prepared to answer questions, defend and promote the cause of the arts in a given area, and frequently serve as an authority on cultural matters.

PHYSICAL DEMANDS AND ENVIRONMENTAL CONDITIONS

Physically, this work is not demanding. However, there may be a good deal of travel involved, as well as required participation in social, community, and fund-raising events. The job requires stamina and mental and emotional endurance.

WHERE TO FIND THESE JOBS

All 50 States have people in these positions, and the Occupational Statement describes the duties included in these particular jobs. In addition to the State agencies, there are also arts and humanities councils, known by that name or others, representing regional areas, municipalities, or counties. All of these hire executives to administer their programs within the designated area. There are also a number of councils, associations, or alliances, made up of groups of museums and/or other cultural institutions, which operate as nonprofit organizations to promote the common interests of their members. These are likely to be headquartered in large cities, but the establishments they represent may be large or small, and located in rural and urban areas throughout a region.

OPPORTUNITIES FOR EMPLOYMENT AND PROMOTION

Obviously, these are not jobs for newcomers to the field. Because of the requirement that Directors have substantial administrative experience, this sort of work is available only to persons who have established reputations in the cultural world.

However, smaller cities with low budgets for this sort of public service could employ bright and energetic recent college graduates in this capacity; and, as more and more cities throughout the country establish arts councils, there should be a number of openings available.

Recent graduates wishing to get into this kind of work might find many opportunities to work as administrative assistants in such agencies. This is especially true of councils in the more heavily populated States and cities, where a number of employees are needed to represent the agencies at functions or in various sections of the State. There is no way of predicting the advancement possibilities for people in these jobs. The personal identification of Directors with the organizations would surely add to their prestige, and make them likely candidates for positions at higher levels; but, in all cases, actual advancement would depend on both the hiring requirements of employing agencies and the individual qualifications and ambitions of the workers.

DIRECTOR, EDUCATION

OCCUPATIONAL STATEMENT

Plans, develops, and administers educational program of museum, zoo, or similar institution: Confers with administrative personnel to decide on scope of program to be offered. Prepares schedules of classes and rough drafts of course content to determine number and background of instructors needed. Interviews, hires, trains, and evaluates work performance of education department staff. Contacts and arranges for services of guest lecturers from academic institutions, industry, and other establishments to augment education staff in presentation of classes. Assists instructors in preparation of course descriptions and informational materials for publicity or distribution to class members. Prepares budget for education programs, and directs maintenance of records of expenditures, receipts, and public and school participation in programs. Works with other staff members to plan and present lecture series, film programs, field trips, and other special activities. May teach classes. May speak before school and community groups and appear on radio or television to promote institution's programs. May coordinate institution's educational activities with those of other area organizations to make greatest use of resources. May train establishment volunteers to assist in presentation of classes or tours. May develop and submit program and activity grant proposals and applications and implement programs funded as a result of successful applications.

EDUCATION, TRAINING, AND EXPERIENCE

The educational requirements for this job vary from an advanced degree in a field related to the institution's specialization to a bachelor's degree in education, museum work, or an appropriate an, science, or history field. Most employers prefer to hire people with experience in teaching or academic administration, either in a museum or a public school or college. Other qualifying work experience might be found in community service or public relations work for a museum or other nonprofit institution. Institutions that offer courses for academic credit by certain colleges and universities are more likely to require Directors, Education, to have an academic administrative background than those that do not. Those that specialize in only one technology or subject area, such as photography, aeronautics, or astronomy, are the most likely to require that their Directors have a strong technical background.

HELPFUL PERSONAL CHARACTERISTICS

Directors, Education, should have good organizational abilities and be able to work effectively with both groups and individuals, in order to plan and implement the institution's program, supervise the education department staff, and coordinate department activities with those of other sections of the institution. Poise and ease in speaking and writing are also important , to represent the institution in public, and to develop appropriate publicity materials.

PHYSICAL DEMANDS AND ENVIRONMENTAL CONDITIONS

This is light work which makes no unusual physical demands on the worker. Public speaking or teaching responsibilities may have to be filled in the evening. Most Education Directors work in comfortable, climate-controlled indoor settings, although some classes, especially those offered by science museums or State or national parks, may be conducted out of doors.

WHERE TO FIND THESE JOBS

Almost every museum, zoo, planetarium, and botanical garden in the country offers some sort of educational program, and the large majority employ Education Directors. Many national and State parks have extensive educational programs and facilities, which are administered by environmental specialists or other civil service personnel.

OPPORTUNITIES FOR EMPLOYMENT AND PROMOTION

Most of these jobs are held by people who have been promoted from other jobs in the same or a similar establishment. However, institutions that stress the importance of a particular technological or academic background frequently hire from the outside. Jobs of this type with the National Park Service or State park systems are held by Park Rangers, historians, naturalists, or interpreters who meet the established civil service requirements. Because of the continuing emphasis on the educational function of museums, there should be more openings for Education Directors as additional establishments are able to broaden their education programs.

Education Directors may advance to higher level administrative posts if they have qualities of leadership and organizational ability, or to curatorial positions if they have intensive training in the appropriate field and are interested in research.

EDUCATIONAL RESOURCE COORDINATOR

OCCUPATIONAL STATEMENT

Directs operation of educational resource center of museum, zoo, or similar institution: Maintains collections of slides, video tapes, programed texts, and other educational materials related to institution's specialty, storing or filing materials according to subject matter, geographic or ethnic association, or historical period. Composes, or directs others in composition of, descriptions of materials, and prepares catalog listing materials, for use of museum staff members, area school teachers, and others. Compiles lists of books, periodicals, and other materials designed to augment items available in resource center. Explains storage and cataloging systems to teachers and others who visit center and suggests materials appropriate for various projects, such as preparing school classes for tour of institution, or presentation of lecture for community group. Issues loan materials to teachers or lecturers, or schedules and coordinates delivery of materials to designated locations. Maintains records of loans and prepares circulation reports for review by Director, Education, or other administrative personnel. Conducts workshops to acquaint area educators with use of institution facilities and materials. Attends teachers' meetings and conventions to promote use of institution's services.

EDUCATION, EXPERIENCE, AND TRAINING

The resource coordinator should have a bachelor's degree in a subject related to the institution's specialty—history, art history, zoology, botany, photography—plus some work experience in a teaching capacity, either in a museum or school. Experience in curriculum planning is especially helpful. Some small or very specialized institutions may hire persons with less formal education for this job, if they are very knowledgeable about the subject matter.

HELPFUL PERSONAL CHARACTERISTICS

Good clerical and organizational abilities are important to maintain records accurately and to group together materials of similar nature so that they can be easily found.

Verbal ability is needed to write clear and concise descriptions of the available materials, and also to explain their use, both to people using the resource center and to those participating in workshops or attending teachers' meetings.

PHYSICAL DEMANDS AND ENVIRONMENTAL CONDITIONS

This is light work that makes no unusual physical demands on the worker.

WHERE TO FIND THESE JOBS

Jobs of this type are found in museums and other institutions in large cities or metropolitan areas, especially in those that offer extensive educational programs in cooperation with public school systems. Although museums in smaller communities may have resource centers and also work with the schools, they usually do not employ any one specifically to operate such a center, but add this responsibility to the job of Teacher or Director, Education.

OPPORTUNITIES FOR EMPLOYMENT OR PROMOTION

Because of the limited number of institutions maintaining large resource centers, there are relatively few opportunities for jobs such as these. However, as more institutions expand their educational programs to include increased cooperation with school systems, more jobs as Educational Resource Coordinators should become available. People employed in these jobs may be promoted to Director, Education, positions.

EXHIBIT ARTIST

OCCUPATIONAL STATEMENT

Produces artwork for use in permanent or temporary exhibit settings of museum, zoo, or similar establishment: Confers with Exhibit Designer, display coordinator, and other personnel to discuss objectives of exhibits and type of artwork needed. Performs any combination of the following duties to prepare exhibit setting and accessories for installation. Makes scale drawing of exhibit design, indicating size, position, and general outlines of artwork needed, for use of installation and other fabrication personnel. Paints scenic, panoramic, or abstract composition on canvas, board, burlap, or other material to be used as background or component of exhibit, following layout prepared by designer. Paints or stencils exhibit titles and legends on boards, or cuts letters from plastic or plywood to form title and legend copy, and mounts letters on panel or board, using adhesives or handtools. Photographs persons, artifacts, scenes, plants, or other objects, and develops negatives to obtain prints to be used in exhibits. Enlarges, intensifies, or otherwise modifies prints, according to exhibit design specifications. Fashions exhibit accessories, such as human figures, tree parts, or relief maps from clay, plastic, wood, fiberglass, papier mache, or other materials, using hands, handtools or molding equipment to cut, carve, scrape, mold, or otherwise shape material to specified dimensions. Brushes or sprays protective or decorative finish on completed background panels, informational legends, and exhibit accessories. May maintain files of photographs, paintings, and accessories, for use in future exhibits. May do artwork, such as wash drawings, pen and ink sketches, and precision lettering, for posters, informational brochures, or other materials published by institution. May also design or install exhibit fittings. May be designated according to special skill, as exhibit photographer, or exhibit painter.

EDUCATION, TRAINING, AND EXPERIENCE

The usual educational requirement for full-time employment in this work is graduation from a university or art institute, with a degree in fine or applied art and specialization in a specific type of art, such as advertising display, commercial art, illustration, photography, or craft design. Some establishments require only that these workers have art training, acquired at a junior college, technical school, or vocational high school.

Familiarity with and skill in all sorts of art techniques are required for most of these jobs, since only very large establishments with numerous employees can afford to hire specialists in each of the kinds of art work involved.

Experience of a year or more as a commercial artist, illustrator, or advertising display developer is preferred, but many establishments will consider talented beginners.

Many establishments do not hire full-time workers for these jobs, but use the services of free-lance commercial artists or art agencies.

HELPFUL PERSONAL CHARACTERISTICS

This artwork differs from that done by the creative artist in that it must support and enhance the objects exhibited, rather than in itself be the center of attention. Exhibit Artists must be able to channel their talent to this purpose, to help explain or promote a scientific, historic, or other display. They should be perfectionists, to produce the desired results, and have the manual skills and dexterity to work quickly and efficiently. Because they may be working on components for several different exhibits at the same time, Exhibit Artists should also be well organized and able to work under some pressures.

PHYSICAL DEMANDS AND ENVIRONMENTAL CONDITIONS

This is light work, which makes no unusual physical demands on the workers. Good eyesight, including near and far acuity, depth perception, accommodation, and color vision, is needed to produce and judge the quality of artwork. The Exhibit Artist works in a well-lit, temperature-controlled studio or workshop.

WHERE TO FIND THESE JOBS

Most Exhibit Artists work for science, natural history, industrial or multi-discipline museums, or planetariums, for these are most likely to feature exhibits requiring special settings and accessories. The National Park Service, at its Interpretive Center at Harpers Ferry, W. Va., employs exhibit specialists to fabricate exhibit materials for installation in park museums or the various visitors' centers. Some art and history museums, zoos, and botanical gardens hire persons for these jobs, but they are more likely to have the occasional work needed done by an outside firm or a free-lance artist, or combine the duties of this job with those of other workers.

OPPORTUNITIES FOR EMPLOYMENT AND PROMOTION

Employment opportunities vary according to the needs of individual hiring establishments. There is always much competition for work in the commercial art field, and this particular kind of commercial art is no exception. Persons who are skilled in all of the requisite techniques and who can present portfolios that include examples of all their skills will receive hiring preference.

Exhibit Artists can advance to the jobs of Exhibit Designer or display coordinator.

Federal civil service jobs in this field require that applicants have both training and experience.

EXHIBIT BUILDER

OCCUPATIONAL STATEMENT

Constructs and installs exhibit structures and fixtures of wood, plywood, fiberglass, and other materials, using handtools and power tools: Studies sketches or scale drawings for temporary or permanent display or exhibit structures, such as framework, fixtures, booths, or cabinets, to determine type, amount, and cost of material needed, and dimensions of structures to be built. Confers with exhibit planning and art personnel to discuss structural feasibility of plans and suggest alternate methods of displaying objects in exhibit. Cuts and shapes specified materials to dimensions, using handtools and power tools. Assembles and fastens parts to construct framework, panels, shelves, and other exhibit components; sprays or brushes paint, enamel, varnish, or other finish on structures; creates special effects by applying finish with cloth, sponge, or fingers to prepare structure for addition of fittings. Mounts fittings and fixtures, such as shelves, panel boards, and shadowboxes, to framework, using handtools or adhesives. Installs electrical wiring, fixtures, apparatus, audiovisual components, or control equipment in framework, according to design specifications. Installs or affixes murals, photographs, mounted legend materials, and graphics in framework or on fixtures. Works with maintenance and installation personnel to move exhibit components and display furniture from workshop, and to assemble and install or arrange structures in exhibit galleries. Tests electrical, electronic, and mechanical components of exhibit structure to verify operation. May maintain inventory of building materials, tools, and equipment, and order supplies as needed for construction of exhibit fixtures. May assign duties to and supervise work of carpenters, electricians, and other craft work-

41

ers engaged in constructing or installing exhibit components. May assist in placement of display accessories and collection objects or specimens. May be designated according to specialty, as exhibit carpenter or exhibit electrician, or job location, as Planetarium Technician, or science center display builder.

EDUCATION, TRAINING, AND EXPERIENCE

Most establishments require that persons hired for this position have extensive previous experience in carpentry or cabinetmaking, and the knowledge, even if not acquired through actual work experience, of other crafts related to construction. In large establishments, where craft specialists, such as carpenters, electricians, audiovisual experts, and others are employed, the need for the Exhibit Builder to be versed in all crafts is less than in smaller organizations, which may require these workers to be jacks-of-all-trades and, preferably, masters of most.

There are no specific educational requirements as the experience and knowledge needed may have been obtained through several combinations of formal education, vocational training, and previous experience.

A few institutions require Exhibit Builders to have some college training in museography — display techniques, diorama preparation, and other technical courses — to give them a greater understanding of their work and prepare them to plan, as well as execute, special display units and exhibit settings.

If students show aptitude for this kind of work, some museums will hire inexperienced graduates of vocational high schools and other technical training institutions as trainee carpenters, electricians, or Audiovisual Technicians. Such workers would receive on-the-job training, either through a government subsidized program or the institution's own employment and training program, in the skills needed for this type of structural work.

HELPFUL PERSONAL CHARACTERISTICS

Exhibit Builders should be interested and skillful in working with their hands, using hand and power tools and equipment, and reading and understanding scale drawings and work specifications.

They should take pride in their work and in their role in assembling and installing the institution's exhibits.

When performing the more complex duties of this job, such as evaluating the practicality of plans for exhibits, or estimating the amount and cost of materials needed to construct various items. Exhibit Builders need common sense, technical expertise, and, especially, creative and imaginative ideas to suggest and devise other innovative and effective exhibit components.

PHYSICAL DEMANDS AND ENVIRONMENTAL CONDITIONS

This is medium to heavy work, requiring that workers lift, carry, and move lumber, other materials, tools and equipment, and finished exhibit and display fixtures and furniture, both in the workshop and in exhibit galleries where the items are installed. Good vision and manual and finger dexterity are important in performing construction duties and evaluating their results.

This is indoor work, performed in a workshop setting.

WHERE TO FIND THESE JOBS

Virtually all museums, zoos, planetariums, parks, and botanical gardens maintain workshops where exhibit materials are stored and structures fabricated or assembled. Exhibit Builders also work for the Federal Government at centers where display and exhibit hardware and components are fabricated for installation in national parks and other sites. These workers may also be employed by firms that specialize in the production of both standard display and exhibit furnishings and equipment, and structures or components specifically designed for framing and displaying special exhibits.

OPPORTUNITIES FOR EMPLOYMENT AND PROMOTION

These vary according to the needs of individual institutions and the qualifications of workers. Museums and similar establishments would like to hire more persons for this kind of work if funds were available because most institutions believe that it's more practical and economical to have exhibit components fabricated in their own workshops than to purchase them from outside sources.

Persons with experience and several structural skills will find this kind of job easier to get than those who are adept in only one craft.

A number of institutions operated by cities or counties use craft workers employed by the local civil service system for this work. They are either assigned to the institution itself, or do structural work for a number of facilities operated by the city or county.

Federal jobs require applicants to meet the qualifications standards and pass the civil service tests for the position of an exhibits specialist.

Openings for this type of work are not likely to be advertised in help wanted columns, although announcements of openings subsidized by Federal or local work/training programs may be published occasionally. Persons who are interested in this kind of work and who have the stated qualifications should inquire at the personnel office of the appropriate institution or the civil service headquarters in their community to find out about employment possibilities.

EXHIBIT DESIGNER

OCCUPATIONAL STATEMENT

Plans, designs, and oversees construction and installation of permanent and temporary exhibits and displays: Confers with administrative, curatorial, and exhibit staff members to determine theme, content, interpretive or informational purpose, and planned location of exhibit: discusses budget, production, and time limitations; plans production schedule for fabrication and installation of exhibit components. Prepares rough drawings of proposed exhibit, including detailed construction, layout, special effects diagrams, and material specifications for final drawing rendition by artist, basing design and specifications on knowledge of artistic and technical concepts, principles, and techniques. Submits plans for approval of other staff members and adapts plans as needed to better serve intended purpose or to conform to budget or fabrication restrictions. Oversees preparation of artwork and construction of exhibit components to assure proper interpretation of concepts and conformance to structural and material specifications. Arranges for acquisition of specimens of graphics or building of exhibit structures by outside contractors as needed to complete exhibit. Inspects installed exhibit for conformance to specifications and satisfactory operation of special effects components. Oversees placement of collection objects or informational materials in exhibit framework.

EDUCATION, TRAINING, AND EXPERIENCE

These workers are almost always required to have at least a bachelor's degree and sometimes a master's, usually in art, with emphasis on design, museography, or graphics. Depending on the emphasis and hiring policies of individual institutions, a degree in architecture, engineering, or museum studies may be either a requirement or an acceptable alternative.

Very few establishments hire inexperienced workers for these jobs, with the possible exception of extremely small operations where the designer is also the artist and the builder.

Exhibit Designers have usually had previous museum experience in exhibit work, or substantial non-museum administrative and technical experience in such fields as advertising, commercial display and exhibit fabrication, or industrial or theatrical design.

All workers in this job are expected to be familiar with such technical processes as diorama fabrication, silk-screen and other graphic art methods, carpentry and other structural craft techniques as well as material, production, and cost factors associated with exhibit fabrication. In addition, they are expected to understand and be able to apply principles of art and design in innovative and appropriate ways.

Designers who work for natural history museums, zoos, or similar establishments may also be required to have experience in taxidermy and familiarity with zoological or anthropological materials; those employed by parks or botanical gardens must be knowledgeable about the long-term display of plants. Designers who work for planetariums must have the most technical knowledge of all, in order to cooperate with astronomers, electrical technicians, and other experts to create sets and special effects for sky shows and other animated exhibits. All designers are expected to have the basic training and experience described in the first paragraphs of this section. Those who work for specialty museums and other institutions are usually expected to have familiarity with, or expertise in, the specific subject matter or techniques related to that specially.

HELPFUL PERSONAL CHARACTERISTICS

Exhibit Designers should be both creative and practical, in order to plan imaginative and attractive exhibits that can be constructed in accordance with established budget and technical limitations.

They also need to be able to get along well with other staff members, both administrators and technicians, to plan and supervise the fabrication of the exhibits.

PHYSICAL DEMANDS AND ENVIRONMENTAL CONDITIONS

This is light work, which makes no unusual physical demands on the worker. It is usually performed in an office or studio setting.

WHERE TO FIND THESE JOBS

Exhibit Designers work for all types of museums, planetariums, some zoos and botanical gardens, commercial exhibit and display fabrication firms, the National Park Service, and certain other Federal, State, and local agencies.

OPPORTUNITIES FOR EMPLOYMENT AND PROMOTION

These are not entry jobs in most establishments; although some small museums will hire recent graduates for exhibit design and construction work, the majority of Exhibit Designers have had substantial experience in the same or a similar institution, and have been promoted to these positions. Persons who are interested in this kind of work should apply for jobs at a lower level, as exhibits technicians, Exhibit

Artists or builders, with the idea of advancing to the more responsible planning and designing positions.

In some large establishments, the duties described for this job are divided between two or more workers, some concerned with planning, some with designing, and some coordinating the construction of exhibits. In all cases, these represent high-level positions, requiring substantial experience and educational preparation. Federal civil service descriptions for the jobs of exhibit planner, production project manager, exhibit planner, production project manager, Exhibit Designer, and interpretive specialist all relate to the Occupational Statement for this job. Information about similar jobs with State or local agencies may be obtained by contacting appropriate civil service offices.

FINE ARTS PACKER

OCCUPATIONAL STATEMENT

Specifies types of packing materials, crating, containerization, and special handling procedures for shipping or storing art objects, scientific specimens, and historical artifacts to minimize damage and deterioration: Confers with curatorial personnel regarding status of museum projects and proposed shipping or transfer dates of exhibitions. Develops methods and procedures for packing or containerization of art objects, according to weight and characteristics of shipment. Selects protective or preservative materials, such as excelsior, chemical agents, or moisture-proof wrapping, to protect shipment against vibration, moisture, impact, or other hazards. Designs special crates, modules, brackets, and traveling frames to meet insurance and museum specifications. Shapes and contours internal support modules, based on size and type of paintings, sculptures, bronzes, glass, and other art objects. Directs workers engaged in moving art objects from receiving storage areas to galleries of museums, in packing shipments, or in rigging sculptures for installation of exhibition. Inspects incoming shipment to detect damage for insurance purposes. Keeps records and documents of incoming and outgoing shipments, or locations of traveling exhibitions and loan materials. Prepares and attaches written or pictorial instructions for unpacking, storage, or exhibition of contents of shipment. May specify type of carrier, such as barge, train, or messenger according to cost consideration and nature of shipment.

EDUCATION, TRAINING, AND EXPERIENCE

This position is usually filled by a person who has had lengthy experience as a packer or crater in a museum or with a firm which

transports museum objects. There is no specific educational requirement for job entry. Workers learn the various methods and materials
used in packing museum objects through experience in subordinate
jobs, through exchange of information with fine arts packer employed
by other institutions, or by studying informational materials provided
by the manufacturers of packing containers or substances. New devel-
opments in packing materials occur frequently, and the Fine Arts Packer
must keep up with these in order to best accommodate the needs of the
institution. In most institutions, these workers are concerned, primarily,
with designating and supervising the packing of objects. Although they
also keep records of incoming and outgoing shipments, the examination of unpacked objects, as well as the maintenance of records concerning items in the collection of the institution and those making up part of
a traveling exhibition, is usually done by the Registrar or another member of the professional staff.

HELPFUL PERSONAL CHARACTERISTICS

Fine Arts Packer should be interested in working with their hands
and willing to do manual work because they are sometimes required to
work right along with the persons they supervise.

In addition, they should be interested enough in their jobs to keep
informed of new packaging containers and materials, and be able to
devise appropriate methods of packing or crating unusually shaped or
exceptionally fragile articles for shipment. They also need good spatial
and form perception, in order to visualize the structural form of the
packing containers needed to accommodate a variety of items.

They should have average clerical skills to maintain shipping and
receiving records.

Depending on the duties in specific positions, Fine Arts Packers
should be able to plan their own activities and those of other persons in
the shipping and receiving departments, and to get along well with the
workers they supervise, other institution staff members, and representatives of the various firms engaged to transport museum objects.

PHYSICAL DEMANDS AND ENVIRONMENTAL CONDITIONS

This work does not demand exceptional strength because Fine Arts
Packers spend most of their time overseeing packing and unpacking
operations, devising methods of packing or crating objects, or keeping
records.

However, these workers should have the manual skill and dexterity needed to assist in the packing and unpacking activities as needed.

Because of the importance of maintaining proper temperature and humidity in any setting where works of art or various artifacts are kept, the shipping departments in these institutions are more pleasant to work in than those of most business or industrial firms.

WHERE TO FIND THESE JOBS

All but the smallest museums employ workers in these jobs. Some large art, history, and science institutions may employ 10 or more Fine Arts Packers, whose duties include advising and assisting in the preparation of containers for storage, as well as shipment, of museum objects.

Although zoos and botanical gardens employ workers to prepare animals and botanical specimens, respectively, for shipment, packing workers in both of these kinds of institutions require specialized skills and knowledge that differ from those demanded by Fine Arts Packers.

OPPORTUNITIES FOR EMPLOYMENT AND PROMOTION

Since workers must learn to pack art objects, artifacts, and historically significant articles and papers on the job, there is no opportunity for newcomers to be hired as Fine Arts Packers, unless they have had extensive experience in this work with a trucking or other kind of transportation firm.

However, there are numerous opportunities for employment in the shipping and receiving departments of museums. Many such positions may be funded by CETA or some other federally funded work/training program.

Persons hired as packers, who show both conscientiousness in performance of their duties and the willingness to learn new methods and techniques, may advance to these relatively responsible positions with a minimum of formal education.

Fine Arts Packers may advance to supervisory positions with large institutions. Since many establishments which employ these workers are operated by local, State, or Federal Government bodies, civil service regulations may permit these workers to advance to other jobs in related fields.

Fine Arts Packers may also go into business for themselves, as consultants who advise museums on the best methods of packing and shipping various objects, or as the operators of carriers that specialize in the transportation of museum or other fine arts objects.

FURNITURE RESTORER

OCCUPATIONAL STATEMENT

Performs any combination of following duties to repair, restore, and preserve period furnishings in collection of museum or similar institution: Examines furnishings to determine condition, material, extent of deterioration or damage, or date of construction, to verify authenticity or plan restorative treatment. Sets up and operates variety of woodworking machines and uses various handtools to fabricate, repair, reinforce, and replace parts of furniture, cutting, shaping, and attaching parts according to blueprints or drawings, and matching materials for color, grain, and texture. Strips old finish from furnishings, using solvents and abrasives. Fills cracks, depressions, and other blemishes, using plastic wood or lacquer stick. Treats warped or stained surfaces to restore original contour and color. Glues or replaces veneer sections. Smooths surfaces, using power sander or abrasive material. Washes, bleaches, or otherwise treats surfaces to prepare for application of finish. Selects appropriate stain, lacquer, varnish, or other coating, and brushes or sprays material onto surface, to protect surface and produce desired appearance. Polishes or waxes finished pieces. Removes damaged or deteriorated coverings from upholstered furniture. Repairs, reinforces, or replaces springs, webbing, padding and other components. Selects fabric for new covering, according to instructions of Curator or knowledge of patterns and material appropriate to period and style of furniture. Tacks, sews, glues, or staples covering to furniture frame to upholster piece. Refurbishes leather coverings of furnishings, using softeners, solvents, adhesives, stains, or polishes, or replaces damaged coverings with pieces cut from leather of appropriate color, grain, and weight. Stencils, gilds, embosses, or paints designs or borders on restored pieces, to reproduce original appearance. May advise curatorial staff on environmental conditions necessary for preservation of furnishings in exhibit and storage areas. May fabricate replicas of period furniture for use in exhibits. May be designated according to specialty, as upholstery restorer or finish specialist.

EDUCATION, TRAINING, AND EXPERIENCE

Furniture Restorers who work for museums, historical communities, and similar institutions may have operated or been employed by commercial antique restoration firms, or may have begun their careers as helpers or assistants in the conservation departments of museums or group-operated laboratories.

Persons with shop training in woodworking, especially if they have also had courses in drafting or commercial art, and those with hobbies or work experience involving refinishing furniture or constructing objects of wood may meet the hiring requirements for trainees or assistants in this field.

Newcomers to the field are given on-the-job training in the techniques of cabinetmaking, upholstering, and refinishing wood. Such training, under experienced workers lasts from 6 to 12 months. At the end of the training period, workers are responsible for their own projects, which become progressively more difficult as they acquire knowledge and experience.

HELPFUL PERSONAL CHARACTERISTICS

Restorers should be interested in working with their hands, using tools and machines skillfully. They should like the feel of wood, and enjoy the challenge of transforming battered, broken furnishings into things of beauty.

These are not jobs for careless people. Furniture Restorers must be able to work patiently and with extreme precision, to repair or restore items ranging in age, fragility, and value, from sturdy 19th-century farm furniture to priceless 16th-century altarpieces.

They should be able to learn the properties of the various materials of which furnishings are made, as well as the most practical methods and agents with which to repair or treat them. An interest in science will help experienced restorers develop innovative methods for using chemicals to condition, restore, and maintain furnishings in their various exhibit and storage environments.

PHYSICAL DEMANDS AND ENVIRONMENTAL CONDITIONS

Most of this is light work, performed in a workshop setting. When working on large articles, Furniture Restorers may have to lift and carry parts of the objects for varying distances, but they are more likely to stand or sit at a worktable for long periods of time. Good eyesight, especially the qualities of near acuity, depth perception, and color vision, is important, as are manual dexterity and coordination.

Workshops may be noisy, because of the operation of machinery and power tools; fumes and mists from solvents, paints, and other coatings are frequently present. However, workers may use earplugs to minimize the effect of the noise, and masks to prevent excessive inhalation of fumes and mists.

WHERE TO FIND THESE JOBS

Large history, art, and multi-emphasis museums employ Furniture Restorers, as do restored homes, communities and farms, and historic or theme parks. A number of persons work for the Federal Government or various State governments in conservation facilities established to restore and preserve furnishings exhibited in their museums and historic structures. Furniture Restorers also work for conservation laboratories, operated commercially or by groups of institutions in the same area or with the same emphasis. Small institutions are not likely to employ Furniture Restorers; when they need these services, they may use one of the numerous firms that specialize in the restoration of fine furniture and antiques, or hire a person employed by a larger institution that permits its workers to accept additional work.

OPPORTUNITIES FOR EMPLOYMENT AND PROMOTION

The number of openings for this kind of work fluctuates according to the expansion of existing facilities and the rate of attrition among persons currently employed.

Continued government support of museums, especially through work/ study and employment and training programs designed to help disadvantaged persons, should make it possible for many institutions to hire more trainees for this kind of work. The experienced Furniture Restorer can almost always find a market for his or her skills, in the museum field, as a free-lance specialist, or as the operator or employee of a commercial restoration firm.

Furniture Restorers may, occasionally, be promoted to head the conservation facilities of museum or commercial laboratories; however, such positions usually require extensive knowledge of the sophisticated techniques used to restore paintings, textiles, paper, and other materials and few Furniture Restorers have this kind of background.

GARDEN WORKER

OCCUPATIONAL STATEMENT

Performs any combination of the following duties to cultivate and care for ornamental plants, install floral displays, and maintain growing and gardening equipment and structures: As directed by supervisory personnel, conditions and prepares soil and plants seeds, seedlings, or bulbs in greenhouse or outdoor growing area; fertilizes, waters, weeds, transplants, or thins plants in growing areas; mixes and applies pesticides to maintain health of plants and to prepare for installation in greenhouse or outdoor display areas; lays sod or artificial grass, and builds framework for indoor floral displays, or prepares outdoor display beds, according to work plan designed by horticulturist, landscape gardener, or other professional personnel; moves plants from growing area and transplants in display beds, or places potted plants in beds according to work plans; tends display beds to maintain health of plants and beauty of display; operates, maintains, and repairs sprayers, sprinklers, cultivators, and other equipment; caulks windows, replaces panes, constructs hot beds, and performs other duties to maintain and repair greenhouse and other facilities. May also mow lawns, prune trees and bushes, and perform other duties to maintain grounds.

EDUCATION, TRAINING, AND EXPERIENCE

Although most persons now employed in this capacity were hired with little or no vocational training, employers now prefer to hire people who have had horticultural training, either in a high school or vocational school, or through previous employment with a commercial nursery or similar institution. In many establishments, workers may start out as landscape laborers or groundskeepers, and be promoted to this type of work, after receiving on-the-job training and becoming familiar with the more advanced techniques involved in growing and caring for plants.

Some institutions hire workers for these jobs through government-subsidized work-training programs; however, persons with some gardening experience are preferred as participants, since it takes a year or so for people with no background in this kind of work to acquire gardening skills.

HELPFUL PERSONAL CHARACTERISTICS

Garden Workers should be interested in working with their hands to make things grow. They should be able to adjust to a work schedule which includes a variety of duties, and be willing to follow instructions of their supervisor and of the other professional and technical personnel that they may be assigned to assist.

As they acquire the skill to perform the more complex duties, they should also be able to make valid decisions concerning appropriate methods of growing and caring for a variety of plants.

They need good spatial and form perception in order to follow the diagrams for the construction of indoor and outdoor floral display beds, lo install specified plants in these beds, and to thin, trim, and prune plants properly.

PHYSICAL DEMANDS AND ENVIRONMENTAL CONDITIONS

This is medium to heavy work, performed indoors in climate-controlled greenhouses or work sheds, and outdoors in the growing and display areas of the institution. Both physical agility and strength are needed, to stoop, squat, and crouch, while cultivating and tending plants, and to lift and carry plants, equipment, and materials for varying distances. Individual positions vary in strength and stamina requirements, but, in most cases, workers should be able to work outdoors in all kinds of weather and to maintain a steady work pace throughout the day.

WHERE TO FIND THESE JOBS

Botanical gardens, arboretums, park systems, zoos, and almost all institutions with extensive grounds and/or floral displays hire Garden Workers. They may also work for commercial nurseries, landscaping service organizations, other public and private institutions, and individuals with large estates.

OPPORTUNITIES FOR EMPLOYMENT AND PROMOTION

There are numerous opportunities for employment in this kind of work, especially for persons who have had some training in horticulture. Many jobs are available through local and State civil service systems. Some of these require only eighth grade education, plus some indication of the ability, either proven or potential, to care for plants. In most localities, workers are hired through civil service and then are assigned to work for a particular institution and receive on-the-job training by its supervisory staff. Other institutions hire Garden Workers directly, and accept applications for employment at their personnel offices.

Work of this kind is also available with the Federal Government, in the National Park Service and with other agencies. Information about such positions may be obtained by filling out a job interest card, available at all Federal Job Information Centers.

Enrollment in a government-sponsored work/study or work/training program may be through the local school system, the community CETA program, or a youth program funded under CETA.

Garden Workers may advance to such positions as grower or Plant Propagator, or to supervisory work with the same establishment.

GROUNDSKEEPER, INDUSTRIAL-COMMERCIAL

OCCUPATIONAL STATEMENT

Maintains grounds of industrial, commercial, or public property, performing combination of following tasks: Cuts lawns, using hand mower or power mower. Trims and edges around walks, flower beds, and walls, using clippers and edging tools. Prunes shrubs and trees to shape and improve growth, using shears. Sprays lawn, shrubs, and trees with fertilizer or insecticide. Rakes and burns leaves and cleans or sweeps up litter, using spiked stick or broom. Shovels snow from walks and driveways. Spreads salt on public passageways. Plants grass, flowers, trees, and shrubs.

Waters lawn and shrubs during dry periods, using hose, or by activating fixed or portable sprinkler system. Repairs fences, gates, walls, and walks, using carpentry and masonry tools. Paints fences and outbuildings. Cleans out drainage ditches and culverts, using shovel and rake. Depending on size and nature of employing establishment, uses tractor equipped with attachments, such as mowers, lime or fertilizer spreaders, and lawn roller. May perform variety of laboring duties, common to type of employing establishment, when yard work is completed.

EDUCATION, TRAINING AND EXPERIENCE

There are no set educational requirements for this job as it is found in institutions of this type. Depending upon the age and the length of employment of incumbents in various settings, the educational level varies from sixth grade or less for older workers who have been employed at the same establishment for a number of years, to high school graduation for persons who have been hired during the last 5 years or so. Ordinarily, inexperienced persons are hired and assigned elementary duties, such as cutting and raking lawns and sweeping and removing litter from paved areas. They are gradually given more responsibility and taught the more complicated duties by experienced workers or supervisory personnel. The tasks performed by workers in this job vary according to the size and facilities of the establishment and the number of groundskeepers employed. For example, the one or two workers employed to maintain the grounds of an historic home perform most of the duties listed, but do so only occasionally because they are responsible for a relatively small area; botanical gardens, zoos, and other institutions with extensive grounds may employ 20 or 30 groundskeepers, some specializing in the care of trees or flowers, others who maintain public areas, and still others who are assigned to repairing and painting fences and outbuildings. Almost all establishments hire inexperienced workers as groundskeepers and train them in the duties for which they are most suited. Many of these jobs are filled through work/study programs of local, State, or Federal agencies.

HELPFUL PERSONAL CHARACTERISTICS

Groundskeepers should enjoy working with their hands, or handtools, in non-industrial, outdoor settings. They should be willing to follow instructions, and be able to adapt to the performance of fairly routine duties on a regular schedule.

PHYSICAL DEMANDS AND ENVIRONMENTAL CONDITIONS

This is medium to heavy work that requires fairly strenuous physical activity and agility. It is performed outdoors in all kinds of weather, although some repair work may be done in a shed or barn when it is extremely cold.

WHERE TO FIND THESE JOBS

Museums, zoos, and similar institutions all employ groundskeepers. The Occupational Statement, Groundskeeper, Parks and Grounds, in this book, describes similar jobs located in city, State, and national parks.

OPPORTUNITIES FOR EMPLOYMENT AND PROMOTION

There are usually many opportunities for both full-time and seasonal employment for this kind of work. Some openings will be filled by participants in work/study or other employment programs sponsored by a government agency, but many more are available to persons who are not eligible for such programs. To apply for employment at institutions operated by cities or counties, inquiries should be made at the appropriate civil service headquarters. Applications for work at privately operated facilities can be made at their personnel offices. Many establishments hire extra workers for these jobs during the summer months, making them attractive to students looking for vacation work. For this temporary work, applications should be made as early as possible, because there is frequently much competition for the jobs.

Full-time groundskeepers can advance to supervisory jobs in the same field. If they have specialized in equipment repair and maintenance, or in caring for flowers and other plants, they may move into more advanced positions in these fields at the same or a similar establishment.

GROUNDSKEEPER, PARKS AND GROUNDS

OCCUPATIONAL STATEMENT

Keeps grounds of city, State, or national parks and playgrounds clean and repairs buildings and equipment: Mows lawns, using handmower or power-driven lawnmower. Grubs and weeds around bushes, trees, and flower beds and trims hedges. Picks up and burns or carts away paper and rubbish. Repairs and paints benches, tables, guardrails, and assists in repair of roads, walks, buildings, and mechanical equipment, using handtools. Cleans comfort stations and other buildings. May live on site and be designated campground caretaker.

EDUCATION, TRAINING, AND EXPERIENCE

For work of this type in most places, there are no stated educational or work experience hiring requirements. The formal education of groundskeepers employed permanently ranges from sixth grade or less to completion of high school. Some park systems cooperate in work/study programs, projects of State or Federal agencies to employ actual or potential high-school dropouts in these jobs, on a full- or part-time basis. Other programs that may provide employment for groundskeepers, both in parks and for the grounds of government and nonprofit-operated institutions are CETA, Youth Conservation Corps (YCC), Veterans Reinstatement Administration, and The Work Incentive Program (WIN). Programs such as these usually include the responsibility, on the part of the employing institution, to give on-the-job training to workers which will help them in future employment. Most of these programs serve people who are underemployed or unemployed. Other employees are usually hired through city or State civil service channels; written examinations may or may not be part of the qualifying process. Information about these jobs in national parks may be obtained from Federal Job Information Centers. Because of heavier public use of parks in summer, there are usually many openings for temporary groundskeepers available to high school and college students. Some of these are filled through government-sponsored summer jobs programs, but there are many more filled by students who apply directly to the appropriate civil service or National Park Service authority. There are no special hiring requirements for summer employment.

HELPFUL PERSONAL CHARACTERISTICS

You should be willing to follow instructions given by supervisory personnel and interested in working outdoors. Many jobs do not require any special skills or knowledge; however, to do well in those involving repairing, painting, and otherwise maintaining park facilities or mechanical equipment, workers should be willing and able to work with their hands, using tools and equipment as required.

PHYSICAL DEMANDS AND ENVIRONMENTAL CONDITIONS

This is medium to heavy work, requiring both stamina and agility. Most jobs are performed outdoors, often in a rustic setting. Groundskeepers should be able to function well working out of doors in extremely hot, cold, or wet weather. In the off season, groundskeepers may spend part of their time painting or repairing equipment in a maintenance shed or garage, but some outdoor work is also done then to prepare premises for public use, or to maintain and refurbish the area after heavy seasonal use. Many jobs of this type require that applicants pass a physical examination prior to employment.

WHERE TO FIND THESE JOBS

Groundskeepers work in city, State, or national parks all over the country. They also are employed by zoos, botanical gardens, and other institutions that have extensive grounds used by the public.

OPPORTUNITIES FOR EMPLOYMENT AND PROMOTION

There should be many opportunities for employment in this kind of work, both full time and temporary. Some of these jobs will be filled by participants in government-subsidized employment programs, but many more, becoming available because of the increased funding of public institutions, should be open through civil service channels. Applications for seasonal employment should be made with the appropriate authorities by March 1, for first consideration. Parks in the South or Southwest may get most of their tourist traffic during the winter months, so more groundskeepers may be needed in these areas from December through March or April. Full-time groundskeepers may advance to supervisory positions; if their duties include extensive building repair or mechanical maintenance work, they may become maintenance mechanics or get into some other sort of structural work. Although temporary groundskeepers cannot be promoted to other jobs, they may find that this part-time experience proves helpful when they apply for full-time work in the same field.

GUARD, MUSEUM

OCCUPATIONAL STATEMENT

Guards property against fire, theft, vandalism, and illegal entry, performing any combination of the following duties: Patrols, periodically, buildings and grounds of museum, zoo, or similar institution. Examines doors, windows, and gates to determine that they are secure. Warns violators of rule infractions, such as loitering, smoking, or carrying forbidden articles, and apprehends or expels miscreants. Inspects equipment and exhibits to ascertain if tampering has occurred. Watches for and reports irregularities, such as fire hazards, leaking water pipes, and security doors left unlocked. Observes departing personnel to guard against theft of property. Sounds alarm or calls police or fire department by telephone in case of fire or presence of unauthorized persons. Permits authorized persons to enter property. May register at watch stations to record time of inspection trips. May record data, such as property damage or unusual occurrences, for use of supervisory staff. May perform janitorial duties and set thermostatic controls to maintain specified temperature in buildings. May tend furnace or boiler. May be deputized to arrest trespassers. May be designated according to area of responsibility, as grounds guard, gallery guard.

EDUCATION, TRAINING, AND EXPERIENCE

Educational requirements for this kind of work vary from the ability to read and write to graduation from high school. There are no uniform experience requirements for all jobs, although most establishments prefer to hire persons with security experience, and many give preference to retired police officers or industrial guards. Training is given to new workers, both experienced and inexperienced, to acquaint them with establishment policies and security equipment operation.

A number of museums and similar institutions contract with a commercial security service firm for provision of Guards, rather than hire workers for these jobs. In these cases, the firm assigns employees to duty at the establishment, and they are responsible both to the security firm and the institution.

Many city-operated institutions employ Guards through the community's civil service system, and applicants must pass a test for hiring consideration.

Almost all Guards, employed by the museum or similar establishment, the community, or a commercial firm, must be able to post security bonds.

HELPFUL PERSONAL CHARACTERISTICS

These vary according to the assignment. Guards who patrol the premises during visiting hours should be able to relate to the public to answer questions about objects on display, as well as to reprimand or take more drastic action against persons who violate rules. Some establishments now give training in public relations to these Guards, as they are the employees most likely to be seen by visitors and, as such, represent the institution.

Guards assigned to night duty, inside an establishment, or to the patrol of extensive outdoor areas, should be able to adjust to working alone, and to following both a specified route and routine without close supervision.

Although all Guards should be able to function well under stress and take strong action when needed, these qualities are more important for those assigned to night duty than for those who work during public visiting hours.

PHYSICAL DEMANDS AND ENVIRONMENTAL CONDITIONS

This is light to medium work, varying according to both the area of responsibility and the method of patrolling that area. In an art museum, for instance, a Guard may be responsible for walking through two or three galleries, while in a zoo or other large outdoor facility, he may patrol several square miles, driving a motor vehicle or even riding horseback. There is some possibility of danger in these jobs because potential thieves or vandals may be surprised and fight apprehension, or groups of visitors may become unruly and cause trouble. Some Guards are required to carry and be able to use firearms or chemical protective devices such as mace, to protect the property for which they are responsible.

WHERE TO FIND THESE JOBS

All institutions of this type have some guard protection, most of them for 24 hours a day. Some smaller establishments, especially those in small communities or rural areas, do not employ Guards as such, but assign this responsibility to other workers during visiting hours and rely on the local police force for after hours protection. However, establishments with collections of value are virtually compelled to hire Guards, as well as to use various other security measures to comply with insurance requirements.

OPPORTUNITIES FOR EMPLOYMENT AND PROMOTION

These vary according to both the employee turnover and the security plans of individual institutions. Establishments that employ round-the-clock Guards usually hire full-time employees to work standard 40-hour weeks, alternating on the three 8-hour shifts. They frequently hire extra workers for weekend duty, or as relief for Guards who are ill or on vacation. There are usually openings for these part-time jobs, which may be available to students, retired persons in good health, or people looking for "moonlight" positions.

Museum Guards may advance to supervisory positions with the same or a similar establishment.

GUIDE, ESTABLISHMENT

OCCUPATIONAL STATEMENT

Escorts a group of people through establishment, such as museum, aquarium, or public or historical building, or through historic or scenic outdoor spot, such as battlefield or cave, usually following specified route: Lectures concerning size, value, and history of establishment, and of specific objects displayed. Points out and explains special properties of features of interest. When employed by establishment devoted to scientific or technical displays, explains scientific theories and facts on which displays are based and demonstrates operation of mechanical or electrical components. Answers questions of group. Assumes responsibility for safety of party. May collect fees from members of party. May solicit patronage. May distribute brochures on establishment or historical site to visitors.

EDUCATION, TRAINING, AND EXPERIENCE

Jobs of this type usually require at least completion of high school. Experience is not specifically required, although any sort of vocational or volunteer activity involved with public contact is extremely helpful. New employees are given training, lasting from a day or two to 2 weeks, to acquaint them with pertinent information about the establishment as well as with data concerning specific objects on display, unusual natural or scientific features, and methods of demonstrating the operation of mechanical or electrical equipment used in exhibits. Both full-time and seasonal Guide jobs are available, the latter usually requiring the shorter training time.

HELPFUL PERSONAL CHARACTERISTICS

Guides should have a genuine liking for people, in order to conduct tours, answer questions, and present information to groups that may include some persons who are rude, unruly, or inattentive. They should also be able to concentrate during training sessions, to absorb all of the information given about the establishment's operating policies, collections, and other features of interest. They need a good memory to retain these facts, plus a strong speaking voice, poise, and enthusiasm, in order to conduct tours that are both enjoyable and educationally worthwhile to establishment visitors.

PHYSICAL DEMANDS AND ENVIRONMENTAL CONDITIONS

The physical requirements for jobs as Guides vary according to the establishment, although all of these positions would be considered light work. Guides in outdoor' historical or natural parks, zoological or botanical gardens, or at the sites of archeological excavations, may drive tour buses or miniature trains over the area, presenting explanations of noteworthy features as they reach them, or stopping periodically to point out certain sections of particular interest. Other Guides conduct tours on foot, at a leisurely pace in pleasant, indoor surroundings, and still others may guide groups up and down rocky footpaths in a western park, or through the damp and dimly lit passages of underground caves. Although seldom thought of as a "physical" requirement, the ability to speak loudly, projecting the voice for sustained period of time, is needed for all jobs of this type.

WHERE TO FIND THESE JOBS

Virtually all museums and similar institutions offer tours of some sort, for special groups or for the general public. However, they do not all employ Guides for this service. In some institutions, Teachers provide tours as part of the educational program. In others, tours are conducted by volunteers. There is no way to generalize about either the type or size of institution most likely to employ Guides because both large and small establishments—art, science, or history oriented—may or may not hire workers for these jobs.

OPPORTUNITIES FOR EMPLOYMENT AND PROMOTION

These vary according to individual establishment policies. Opportunities for full-time, part-time, or temporary work of this kind are available at various establishments.

Full-time work is most likely to be found at large, multi-discipline museums in metropolitan areas, or at larger historic community establishments, where admission is charged and extensive services are offered. Part-time work is most often available at art or history museums that offer tours of the premises at specified times, rather than periodically through the day as enough visitors gather to form a group. Temporary jobs may be found at establishments that have heavy tourist traffic during a particular season, rather than all year round. People interested in this type of work should inquire at individual institutions to find out what their needs and hiring requirements are.

Park guides, who work at national historic or recreational sites, must pass the Federal Assistant examination to be eligible for hiring consideration.

Depending on individual institution policies, Guides may be promoted to supervisory positions, or to other people-oriented jobs, such as volunteer coordinator or tour scheduler, in the same establishment.

HERBARIUM WORKER

OCCUPATIONAL STATEMENT

Fumigates, presses, and mounts plant specimens, and maintains collection records of herbarium operated by botanical garden, museum, or other institution: Records identification information concerning incoming plant specimens. Places specimens in fumigation cabinet

61

and turns valves to release toxic fumes that destroy insects, fungus, or parasites adhering to specimens. Arranges specimens between sheets of unsized paper so that upper and under portions of leaves, blossoms, and other components are visible, and pads papers with layers of felt and newsprint to protect specimens and form stacks. Places specified number of stacks in pressing frame, writing identification information on top layer of paper on each stack, and secures frame around stacks by tightening frame sections with screws, fastening with leather straps, or tying with twine, to compress stacks and press and dry specimens in desired configuration. Mounts dried specimens on heavy paper, using glue, adhesive strips, or needle and thread, and taking care to prevent distortion or breakage of specimens. Writes identification information on papers and inserts mounted specimens in properly labelled envelopes or folders. Files folders in drawers or cabinets according to standard botanical classification system. Maintains card files of specimens in herbarium collection and records of acquisitions, loans, exchanges, or sales of specimens. May be designated according to specialization as plant mounter or exchange and loans clerk.

EDUCATION, TRAINING, AND EXPERIENCE

Some formal education in botany, including courses in botanical taxonomy, is usually required for this job. This may have been acquired in high school, but is most likely received at a college level. Work experience is not required by most employers.

New Herbarium Workers receive on-the-job training from experienced co-workers or supervisory personnel. The tasks of fumigating, drying, and mounting plant specimens can be mastered by most workers in a month or two, but it takes much longer for them to learn to identify and classify any but the most common plant specimens. Herbarium administrators are always interested in hiring persons with more extensive education or experience in plant classification and preservation, but such a background is a bonus, rather than an established hiring requirement.

HELPFUL PERSONAL CHARACTERISTICS

Herbarium Workers should be interested in work with much variety, since they must be able to learn to do several very different things. However, unlike many jobs composed of varied duties, this kind of work is not hectic, and there is little pressure on the worker to meet deadlines, or to switch frequently or rapidly from one set of tasks to another.

Skill with the hands, and the ability to do precise and meticulous work are required to arrange plant specimens properly for drying, and to mount them so that all important parts are visible.

Verbal aptitude is needed to read and understand technical materials related to botanical taxonomy, to learn to identify various genera and species of plants and to accurately record their names and places of origin. Clerical ability is necessary to maintain herbarium records.

PHYSICAL DEMANDS AND ENVIRONMENTAL CONDITIONS

This is light work, making no unusual physical demands on the worker. It is performed indoors. In some herbariums, workers may be exposed to the constant odor of chemical agents used to prevent damage to plant specimens from insects or mildew. However, in the newer premises, air-tight storage facilities prevent the odor from getting into work areas.

WHERE TO FIND THESE JOBS

Many botanical gardens, arboretums, and science museums operate herbariums, as do the botany departments of some universities.

OPPORTUNITIES FOR EMPLOYMENT AND PROMOTION

Because there are relatively few herbariums in the country, there is a much smaller demand for Herbarium Workers than for persons to fill other jobs described in this book. Openings are usually filled by former high school or college botany students who have become aware of herbariums through their classes, and who may have used their facilities to do research.

Herbarium Workers can advance to the positions of herbarium Curator or director, if they continue their studies to acquire advanced degrees. In some small herbariums, non-degreed persons may become managers of the facilities, but this would be an exception to the usual procedures.

HISTORIC SITE ADMINISTRATOR

OCCUPATIONAL STATEMENT

Manages operation of historic structure or site; as directed by governing body, performs any combination of following duties to manage operation of structure or site: Discusses house or site operation with governing body representatives to form or change policies. Oversees activities of building and grounds maintenance staff and of any other employees. Maintains roster of volunteer guides and contacts volunteers to conduct tours of premises according to schedule. Conducts tours, explaining points of interest and answering visitors' questions. Studies documents, books, and other materials to obtain information concerning history of structure or site. Conducts classes in tour presentation methods for volunteer guides. Accepts group reservations for house tours and special social events. Arranges for refreshments, entertainment, and decorations for special events. Collects admission and special event fees, and maintains records of receipts, expenses, and number of persons served. Assists in planning publicity and arranges for printing brochures or placing information in media. Inspects premises for evidence of deterioration and need for repair, and notifies governing body of such need. Makes minor repairs of facilities.

EDUCATION, TRAINING, AND EXPERIENCE

Most employers require that Historic Site Administrators have at least a bachelor's degree in history, preferably with emphasis on the historical period related to the structure or site involved. Some may also require that job candidates have business or management experience. Possible alternates to the history major are bachelor's degrees in museum studies, art history, or one of the humanities, especially if job candidates have had experience in museum collection management, exhibit planning, fund raising, or related work.

Historic Site Administrators may perform a variety of duties and work for an organization having anywhere from no additional employees to 30 or more. For positions which involve the supervision of a number of other workers, administrative experience is important. For those in which the administrator has total responsibility, an academic background in history, museum training, plus demonstrated organizational ability are needed, with or without work experience. The board of governors of historic homes situated in small communities frequently hire recent college graduates as administrators. However, experienced workers are preferred when they are available for the remuneration offered. In fact, a number of Historic Site Administrators accept lodging in the structure as part of their yearly salaries. This practice provides dual benefits: The hiring organization secures the services of an on-premise watchman as well as an administrator, and the worker eliminates housing and transportation costs from financial requirements.

HELPFUL PERSONAL CHARACTERISTICS

Like the hiring requirements listed above, these, too, vary according to the individual position, but not so much in type as in degree. For all jobs of this kind, organizational ability is needed, to plan one's own activities and those of others, whether they be employees or volunteers.

Although research is involved when materials to uncover histori-cal facts are studied or renovation of the premises planned, these are primarily people-oriented jobs that require the worker to get along well with other workers, the members of the governing body and volunteer guides, and the public.

Depending on the individual position, administrators may need both numerical and clerical abilities to prepare budgets and maintain records; creative instincts to plan and outline publicity materials and fund-raising campaigns; technically knowledgeable backgrounds, both to evaluate the physical condition of the buildings and to suggest ap-propriate renovation techniques; and boundless energy and adaptabil-ity, to perform the variety of tasks necessary to the total operation of a historic structure.

PHYSICAL DEMANDS AND ENVIRONMENTAL CONDITIONS

Generally, this is light work which requires no unusual physical activity. However, individual positions differ in their strength re-quirements, and many Historic Site Administrators spend a good deal of their time on their feet, conducting tours, inspecting the premises, or even doing maintenance and repair work.

WHERE TO FIND THESE JOBS

Historic Site Administrators work in large and small communities all over the country, as well as at historic sites maintained by local, State, and Federal Government agencies. The largest number are prob-ably employed by State or country historical societies, which operate many restored homes.

OPPORTUNITIES FOR EMPLOYMENT AND PROMOTION

As more people become conscious of our national heritage and the need to preserve it, there should be more and more structures set aside as historic buildings. Organizations such as the National Trust for His-toric Preservation, the Society for the Preservation of Antiquities, and the American Association for State and Local History promote public interest in historic buildings, and should be able to supply information, on a national level, about employment possibilities. State, county, and local historic societies can provide details about opportunities in their immediate areas. For all jobs with the Federal Government (primarily with the National Park Service), civil service requirements must be met.

There is little opportunity for advancement from these jobs to others with the same organization, except where several structures are operated by the same agency. In these, the administrator of a small establishment may be promoted to a similar job in a larger, or more frequently visited, structure, whose administration is more complex. Persons with this kind of work background may also become executive officers of State historical societies or, when employed by the government, advance to jobs with a higher civil service classification.

INSTALLER

OCCUPATIONAL STATEMENT

Moves, installs, and stores paintings, statuary, and other art objects in art museum: Places protective pads on handtruck platform and lifts paintings, statuary, or other art objects onto handtruck and places protective pads between and around objects to insure against damage. Pushes handtruck from shipping-receiving area to storage or display gallery as directed by supervisor. Places objects to be stored in designated sections of storage area. Removes objects to be displayed from handtruck, hangs paintings, and positions statuary and other objects in cabinets or on stands as directed. Dismantles exhibit components, as directed, and moves art objects, cabinets, and other display items to storage area. Moves designated objects from storage area to shipping room. (May also dust or polish art objects on display, inspect fumigant or preservative containers and temperature and humidity controls in storage areas, replenish supplies and adjust controls as needed, cut cardboard mat blanks to specified dimensions, or perform other duties as directed by Curator, or Exhibit Designer.)

EDUCATION, TRAINING AND EXPERIENCE

No specific educational or experience background is required for this job, although most museums prefer to hire high school graduates. Because of the value and fragility of the objects being handled, past experience in warehouse work is not considered especially helpful. Most museums prefer to hire inexperienced workers and train them in the methods needed to safely move and handle valuable and often delicate objects. A number of museums cooperate with high schools and junior colleges in work/study programs, through which students are employed part time and are taught the skills which could prepare them for full-time work after graduation.

HELPFUL PERSONAL CHARACTERISTICS

Installers should be able to recognize the value of paintings, statuary, china, artifacts, and other objects and use extreme and constant care when moving and handling them to avoid breaking, scratching, or otherwise damaging them. Although any job involving moving and storing items requires that the worker take precautions against breakage, in most cases no critical problems would arise if accidental damage occurred; however, work of this kind in a museum demands the greatest caution on the part of the worker because objects damaged or broken may be irreplaceable and valued at thousands of dollars. The duties, otherwise, merely require the ability to follow directions closely, and to work as part of a crew in installing or dismantling exhibits. Because most museums display less than 25 percent of their collection at any one time, and the remainder must be carefully stored to prevent deterioration or damage, care in placing items in the designated storage areas and in inspecting and correcting environmental controls is also very important.

PHYSICAL DEMANDS AND ENVIRONMENTAL CONDITIONS

This is physically demanding work, requiring strength to lift and carry items weighing up to 100 pounds and to push handtrucks loaded with objects over museum shipping, storage, and display areas; and agility to climb ladders and balance on scaffolding while hanging large paintings or tapestries, to crouch or stoop when arranging articles on handtrucks or placing them in storage cabinets, and to guide loaded handtrucks around corners and through narrow museum passages. Manual and finger dexterity are needed to dust or polish items carefully and thoroughly and to perform other duties, such as using small knives to cut mats to size. The work is performed in all of the environmentally controlled areas of the museum (galleries, passageways, and storage vaults) as well as in the shipping and receiving rooms.

WHERE TO FIND THESE JOBS

Museums all over the country hire people for these positions. In some establishments, Installers may also perform general maintenance duties.

OPPORTUNITIES FOR EMPLOYMENT AND PROMOTION

Most museums would hire more people for this kind of supportive work if more funds were available. Increased government support of the arts, plus participation by museums in work/training programs should permit more hiring of Installers and other such nonprofessional workers. Depending on the organization and size of various institutions, Installers may advance to more responsible positions in museum maintenance, storage, or exhibit installation work.

LABORATORY ASSISTANT, ZOO

OCCUPATIONAL STATEMENT

Assists Zoo Veterinarian or other professional workers in examination and treatment of animals and performance of research: Prepares treatment room for examination of animals and holds or restrains animals during examination, treatment, or inoculation. Hands instruments and materials to veterinarian as directed. Sterilizes and cleans instruments. Administers immunization inoculations to animals to comply with quarantine regulations or to assist in preventive medicine program. Performs routine laboratory tests such as urinalyses and blood counts, according to established procedures. Prepares vaccines and serums, according to standard laboratory methods, and bottles and stores materials for future use. Assists veterinarian in performance of autopsies. Maintains records of preventive and therapeutic treatment administered. Assists veterinarian and other professional personnel in performance of tests and maintenance of records associated with various research projects.

EDUCATION, TRAINING, AND EXPERIENCE

Most laboratory assistants in zoos are hired on the basis of their knowledge of accepted laboratory procedures, which may have been acquired in junior college, technical school, or a high school which offered extensive laboratory sessions in conjunction with classroom training in biology and chemistry. Although experienced workers are always preferred, many zoos consider recent graduates for such jobs. New laboratory assistants are given on-the-job training by the persons they are replacing or by the veterinarian. At first, they perform elementary duties; then, as they gain experience and confidence, they take on increasingly complex tasks and finally assume all of the responsibilities of the job.

HELPFUL PERSONAL CHARACTERISTICS

Zoo Laboratory Assistants should enjoy working with animals to heal and care for them. Even though this is only a part of the job, the ability to handle, soothe and control a wide variety of animals is critical in determining whether a new laboratory assistant will succeed.

These workers must be precise and meticulous in following laboratory procedures to perform tests, prepare serum according to formulas, and maintain records.

Laboratory assistants should be able to work calmly under stress, since animals receiving treatment may react violently. They must also be able to stand the sight of blood when assisting in the treatment of wounds or the performance of surgery or autopsies.

PHYSICAL DEMANDS AND ENVIRONMENTAL CONDITIONS

This is light work, performed in pleasant indoor surroundings. No unusual physical demands are made of the worker, except for the occasional need to help other workers to subdue animals during examination or treatment.

WHERE TO FIND THESE JOBS

This kind of work is found at large zoos and aquariums that employ full-time veterinarians and maintain laboratory, surgery, and autopsy facilities. Smaller zoos usually rely on outside commercial laboratories for testing and assign Animal Keepers to care for quarantined, ill, and injured animals.

OPPORTUNITIES FOR EMPLOYMENT AND PROMOTION

In some zoos, Animal Keepers are promoted to this work if they have the necessary laboratory training. In others, hiring is done through application at the personnel office or through civil service channels. Persons interested in this kind of work should inquire at the personnel office of the establishment to find out about hiring procedures and the possibility of openings.

There are no direct promotional possibilities from this job to others.

LANDSCAPE ARCHITECT

OCCUPATIONAL STATEMENT

Plans and designs development of land areas for projects, such as parks and other recreational facilities, airports, highways, parkways, hospitals, schools, subdivisions, and commercial, industrial, and residential sites: Confers with clients, engineering personnel, and architects on overall program. Compiles and analyzes data on such site conditions as geographic location, soil, vegetation, and rock features, drainage, and location of structures for preparation of environmental impact report and development of landscaping plans. Prepares site plans, working drawings, specifications, and cost estimates for land development, showing ground contours, vegetation, location of structures, and such facilities as roads, walks, parking areas, fences, walls, and utilities, coordinating arrangement of existing and proposed land features and structures. Inspects construction work in progress to insure compliance with specifications, to approve quality of work and materials, and to advise construction personnel and client on landscape features. May be designated according to project as park-landscape architect.

EDUCATION, TRAINING, AND EXPERIENCE

The established educational background for a career in this field is graduation from an accredited university with a bachelor's degree in landscape architecture. Courses included in the curriculum are concerned with both the scientific and technical aspects of the work—horticulture, soil improvement, and land management, for example—and its business and administrative aspects.

HELPFUL PERSONAL CHARACTERISTICS

The Landscape Architect should be interested in applying scientific and technical knowledge to solve individual landscaping problems.

Excellent verbal and numerical aptitudes are needed to understand and benefit from the courses which must be taken, and to prepare working drawings, specifications, and reports.

Spatial and form perception, as well as the ability to do precision work, are also important qualities because the Landscape Architect must be able to visualize designs for the project, basing his plans on compatibility with the features of the area involved, and translating these concepts into precise and easy-to-follow blueprints. Landscape Architects should also have a creative imagination, in order to produce plans which are not only functional, but also esthetically pleasing and appropriate for their purpose.

PHYSICAL DEMANDS AND ENVIRONMENTAL CONDITIONS

This is light work, making no unusual physical demands on the worker. Although Landscape Architects spend some time surveying the area for which plans will be made and inspecting work in progress, most of their working hours are spent indoors.

WHERE TO FIND THESE JOBS

Landscape Architects are employed by the National Park Service, some State and city park systems, and by certain large zoos, botanical gardens, and other facilities. Smaller institutions contract with a firm or individual providing such services. Most Landscape Architects are either self-employed or associated with a landscape contracting or designing firm, or a similar organization.

OPPORTUNITIES FOR EMPLOYMENT AND PROMOTION

Persons graduating with a degree in this field usually have no trouble finding employment; however, they are more likely to be hired by a commercial enterprise than by a government agency or nonprofit institution, whose Landscape Architects must usually be responsible for planning and designing entire projects. Commercial firms often hire recent graduates and assign them to work with more experienced Landscape Architects, gradually giving them more responsibilities.

LIBRARIAN, SPECIAL LIBRARY

OCCUPATIONAL STATEMENT

Manages library containing specialized materials for museum, zoo, or similar institution: Selects, orders, catalogs, and classifies special collections of books, periodicals, and other materials relating to subject emphasis of institution. Searches subject literature, compiles accession lists, and annotates or abstracts material. Assists patrons in research problems. Translates or orders translation of materials from foreign languages into English. Organizes and cares for rare and valuable library holdings. Organizes and manages program to exchange holdings with libraries of similar institutions. Consults with institution administrative and curatorial staff to determine departmental needs. Trains and supervises personnel assigned to library duties. May be designated according to subject matter or employing institution as art librarian (library); history librarian (library); zoo librarian (library); botanical garden librarian (library).

EDUCATION, TRAINING, AND EXPERIENCE

Although a master's degree in library science is the accepted educational requirement for professional librarians (as stated by the American Library Association) not all librarians in these kinds of jobs have this degree. In fact, they are just as likely to have a bachelor's or master's degree in a field related to the institution's specialty, with a few courses in library work included before or after graduation. Librarians in art museums may have degrees in art or art history; those in history or science museums may have majored in American history or in a physical or biological science; and botany or zoology graduates may have jobs as librarians in botanical or zoological gardens.

Most of these workers start as Library Assistants in the same or a similar library, where they are trained in library accession and classification techniques. They may be promoted to librarian after 6 months or 2 years of on-the-job training. Museum Interns may also be assigned to library work, thereby receiving both the training and work experience needed to qualify for library positions in the same or a similar institution.

Many administrators believe that professional training in librarianship is desirable, but the knowledge of the subject matter emphasized by the institution is more important, especially in a small to medium-sized library whose primary emphasis is on the collections owned by the institution. Institutions with large libraries are more likely to hire professionally trained librarians to direct their operations, and to employ other persons, with training and knowledge in appropriate art, science, or history fields, as assistants.

HELPFUL PERSONAL CHARACTERISTICS

Librarians should be both people- and information-oriented. They must be knowledgeable about materials available, but such knowledge is acquired so that it can be passed, either orally or through information in catalogs or files, to persons who are planning exhibits, working research projects, or performing other duties, either as staff members or as visitors to the institution.

For this kind of library work, deep interest in the subject matter is important, so that the librarian can suggest acquisition of appropriate materials, and give authoritative advice to persons using the facility.

For all library work, neatness counts. This phrase reflects the need for organizational and clerical skills, as well as for a temperament that adapts easily and cheerfully to following firmly established procedures for classifying, storing, issuing, and retrieving library properties.

PHYSICAL DEMANDS AND ENVIRONMENTAL CONDITIONS

This is sedentary work, performed in pleasant, well-lit indoor settings. No unusual physical demands are made on the worker.

WHERE TO FIND THESE JOBS

Almost every museum has a library, as do all historical society headquarters, and many zoological and botanical gardens. However, these facilities vary greatly in both size and use, some of them open only to institution staff members or persons engaged in scholarly research, some available to members of the organization which supports the institution, and relatively few open to the general public. Many national and State parks and monuments also have library facilities, containing books, periodicals, manuscripts, and other materials related to the historical, archeological, or natural significance of the sites.

OPPORTUNITIES FOR EMPLOYMENT AND PROMOTION

Because of the variety in size and use of libraries in this sort of institution, there are probably many more libraries than librarians. In institutions where libraries are used only by staff members, their operation may be part of the duties of other workers. The libraries of some other facilities, especially small historical societies, may be operated by volunteers. Persons interested in library work, particularly those who have had formal education in an appropriate field, should contact those institutions where they would like to work even if they do not know whether there are library facilities. Chances are very good that there are and that job inquiries may be welcome from qualified applicants who have the ingenuity to seek them out. Information about civil service requirements for State or Federal library work may be obtained by contacting the superintendent of the facility where jobs may be found.

LIBRARY ASSISTANT

OCCUPATIONAL STATEMENT

Compiles records, sorts, shelves, issues, and receives books, photographs, periodicals, and other materials: Records identifying data on cards to issue library materials to institution staff members and other patrons. Inspects returned materials for damage, and notifies librarian of need for repair or replacement of materials. Reviews records to compile list of materials issued to library users and contacts borrowers to remind them to return materials to library. Sorts materials returned or left on study tables according to classification code, and stores or shelves materials in designated areas. Locates books and other materials for patrons. Issues borrower's identification cards to non-staff members providing proof of permission to use library facilities. Files catalog and identification cards according to established procedures. Repairs books and other materials, using mending tape, adhesive, and brushes. Answers inquiries on telephone or in person, referring persons requiring professional assistance to librarian. May compile information on library materials, prepare catalog cards for materials, and integrate cards into file, assigning classification numbers and descriptive headings according to standard procedures. May classify library materials for use of patrons.

EDUCATION, TRAINING, AND EXPERIENCE

There are several kinds of education and work experience which are considered qualifying for this kind of work. There are also two sets of duties, one of which requires more academic preparation than the other. Library Assistants who shelve, issue, and repair books and other items, and compile circulation records are usually required to be high school graduates. However, high school dropouts may also be considered for this kind of work in many institutions. They may be hired directly by the personnel department or may come to the institution through CETA (Comprehensive Employment and Training Act), a work/study program, or some other employment and training project administered by a Federal, State, or local government agency. Library Assistants in this category receive on-the-job training for 6 months to a year and, if participating in a job project, may or may not be retained as employees when the project is terminated.

Other Library Assistants perform all of the duties mentioned above and also assign classification numbers and descriptive headings to library acquisitions, prepare summaries and reference lists, and perform other duties. For this kind of work, employers usually require that applicants have a bachelor's degree in a field related to the institution's specialization, an associate's degree (earned at an accredited college), in an appropriate field, or some other academic or employment background through which they have obtained subject matter knowledge and/or familiarity with library classification techniques.

HELPFUL PERSONAL CHARACTERISTICS

Library Assistants should enjoy meeting people and be able to maintain a pleasant and poised manner when dealing with library patrons. They should be able to express themselves well, both orally and in writing, to answer questions clearly, and to prepare summarized information. Clerical aptitude is important in the proper maintenance of records. Library Assistants who perform the more complex job duties should enjoy doing research to obtain information about library holdings, and have the ability to write clear and concise summaries of material researched.

PHYSICAL DEMANDS AND ENVIRONMENTAL CONDITIONS

This is light work, usually performed in a pleasant, well-lit setting. Physical agility is needed to bend, stoop, squat, reach, and climb ladders when shelving and storing books and other materials. Good eyesight is an asset because of the amount and kinds of reading involved.

WHERE TO FIND THESE JOBS

Library Assistants work in all but the smallest libraries operated by museums and similar institutions.

OPPORTUNITIES FOR EMPLOYMENT AND PROMOTION

Opportunities for this kind of work vary according to the size and the location of institutions and their operating budgets. Most large institutions would hire more workers for this job if funds were available, but they consider some of the positions expendable when budgets must be cut. Library Assistants who enter the field after high school and stay with the organization can be promoted to the higher level assistantships if they acquire the technical and subject matter expertise needed. College-trained assistants can be promoted to librarian, classified, or cataloger.

MANAGER, RETAIL STORE

OCCUPATIONAL STATEMENT

Manages museum or similarly related retail store engaged in selling specific line of establishment merchandise, performing the following duties personally or supervising employees performing duties: Plans and prepares work schedules and assigns employees to specific duties. Formulates pricing policies on merchandise according to requirements for profitability of store operations. Coordinates sale promotion activities and prepares, or directs workers preparing, merchandise displays and advertising copy. Performs or supervises employees engaged in sales work, taking of inventory, reconciling cash with sales receipts, keeping operating records, or preparing daily record of transactions for accountant. Orders merchandise or prepares requisitions to replenish merchandise on hand. Insures compliance of employees with established security, sales, and record-keeping procedures and practices.

EDUCATION, TRAINING, AND EXPERIENCE

The usual hiring requirements for positions of this type are high school graduation and some retail experience. Such experience should include buying merchandise and keeping inventory and financial records. In many institutions, the Store Manager is the only paid employee, and supervises a staff of volunteers who serve as salespersons. Often, the manager has been a member of this volunteer staff who, having gained experience in the shop, and being familiar with both the establishment's operating policies and buying sources, decides to switch from a volunteer worker to a paying position. Other qualifying experience may have been in a managerial role in a gift shop, craft and hobby shop, or art supply store, or as a buyer for a department store book, gift, or jewelry department.

HELPFUL PERSONAL CHARACTERISTICS

Store Managers should be well organized, efficient, and business oriented to plan and coordinate staffing, ordering, selling, and record-keeping activities. They should enjoy working with people, and be able to get along well with persons of all levels of intelligence and background because they must work with members of the institution staff, the governing body, representatives of firms from which merchandise is purchased and often volunteer salespersons and shop customers.

They should have good verbal and numerical skills to maintain inventory and financial records, order and price merchandise, and prepare reports.

When assigning duties to volunteer salespersons and supervising their work the Store Manager in institutions of this kind must be tactful and diplomatic, as the relationship between manager and salespeople is not the usual bossworker one. Technically, the managers of shops staffed by volunteers are supervising the work of the people who hired them.

PHYSICAL DEMANDS AND ENVIRONMENTAL CONDITIONS

This is light work, performed in pleasant indoor surroundings, that makes no unusual physical demands on the worker.

WHERE TO FIND THESE JOBS

Almost every museum, zoo, and similar institution operates a retail store. In fact, a number of the large institutions have several shops on the premises; some sell gifts, others books, and some sell items closely related to the objects displayed in the institution or to its geographic location.

OPPORTUNITIES FOR EMPLOYMENT AND PROMOTION

A few museum shops are staffed and managed by members of volunteer groups, but most institutions hire paid workers for both managerial and sales positions. This is because such shops are expected to be profitable and add to the financial resources of the institution, rather than to be simply token services; museum management has found that, devoted as volunteers may be, they cannot be as dependable or knowledgeable about operations as are paid workers who staff the shops on a full-time basis.

Opportunities for employment depend on the turnover for this job in institutions that currently have shops managed by paid employees and also on changes in operating policy in establishments whose shops are now managed by volunteers. Inquiries concerning hiring needs and policies may be made at the personnel office of specific institutions.

There is little opportunity for advancement from this job to others in the same institution, except in very large establishments that operate several shops; in these, the manager of one shop may be promoted to a position involving the administration of all the retail facilities of the institution.

MEMBERSHIP SECRETARY

OCCUPATIONAL STATEMENT

Compiles and maintains membership lists, records receipt of dues and contributions, and gives information to members of museum's supportive organization: Compiles and maintains membership lists and contributions records. Welcomes new members and issues membership cards. Explains privileges and obligations of membership, discusses organization problems, adjusts complaints, and gives information to members. Types and sends notices of dues. Collects and records receipts of dues and contributions. Sends newsletters, promotional materials, and other publications to persons on mailing lists. (May compile financial reports for presentation at organization meetings; may attend organization meetings, participate in discussions, and take minutes; may work with organization and museum staff members to plan and organize social or fund-raising events, such as dinners, balls, auctions, or cruises, and maintain records of expenditures and receipts for such events).

EDUCATION TRAINING, AND EXPERIENCE

There are no established hiring requirements for these jobs, although experience in general office work, especially in jobs involving working with figures, is desirable, as is the ability to type. Frequently, persons hired to do this kind of work have been members of the supportive organization and have both knowledge of and familiarity with operating policies of the museum and the organization. Many Membership Secretaries work for both the organization and the museum, their salaries coming from funds raised or dues paid by organization members. Depending on the size of the museum and the number of members of the organization, this may be either a part-time or full-time job.

HELPFUL PERSONAL CHARACTERISTICS

To perform the wide variety of duties included in this job, the Membership Secretary should be both versatile and adaptable. The ability to get along well with people at all levels is important in maintaining pleasant relationships with museum staff and organization members. However, this represents only one major aspect of the job. Membership Secretaries must also be capable of doing careful and accurate work to maintain files, collect and record monies received, and send publications to members according to a sometimes erratic schedule.

In addition to better than average verbal and mathematical skills, probably the most important quality that a successful Membership

Secretary should have is the ability to shift attention from one type of activity to another without losing efficiency: for instance, performing basically clerical duties such as filing, typing, and recording figures with frequent interruptions by the telephone or personal visits from organization members. Diplomacy, tact, and knowledge of all museum functions are also important qualities for these workers to have.

PHYSICAL DEMANDS AND ENVIRONMENTAL CONDITIONS

With few exceptions, this is light work, performed in pleasant indoor surroundings, and makes no unusual physical demands on the worker. When Membership Secretaries attend organization meetings or arrange social functions, they may have to work extra hours and travel to locations some distance from the museums; however, such activities are unusual, and most Membership Secretaries spend their time in the museum membership office, working according to a regular schedule.

WHERE TO FIND THESE JOBS

Jobs of this type are most likely to be found in medium to large institutions with strong supportive organizations. Almost every museum, zoo, and similar establishment in the country has an active organization of volunteers or support personnel, some with active memberships of 1,000 or more. In those with membership rosters of 300 or more, there may very well be several workers in jobs serving members' needs. Smaller establishments, which may have support organizations with fewer than 100 members, may not hire anyone specifically for this job as the duties could be assumed by other employees.

OPPORTUNITIES FOR EMPLOYMENT AND PROMOTION

As institutions work to increase the size of their supportive organizations, there should be continued demand for Membership Secretaries. These workers may advance to higher level administrative jobs in the same institution, or may go into managerial or administrative work with other nonprofit organizations in the community.

MUSEUM ATTENDANT

OCCUPATIONAL STATEMENT

Manages operation of museum and provides information about regulations, facilities, and exhibits to visitors: Opens museum at designated hours, greets visitors, and invites visitors to sign guest register. Monitors visitors viewing exhibits, cautions persons not complying with museum regulations, distributes promotional materials, and answers questions concerning exhibits, regulations, and facilities. Arranges tours of facility for schools or other groups, and schedules Guide or other volunteer or staff member to conduct tours. Examines exhibit facilities and collection objects periodically and notifies museum professional personnel or governing body when need for repair or replacement is observed. May wash windows, clean floors and exhibit cases, dust or wash collection objects, and perform other maintenance duties. May collect admission fees and issue tickets to visitors.

EDUCATION, TRAINING, AND EXPERIENCE

In many cases, the Museum Attendant is the only person employed by the institution. The attendant is hired by the governing body, which establishes operating policies, manages finances, and provides volunteer workers to perform curatorial, administrative, and other duties. Although college graduates are preferred for these positions, high school graduates are often considered, especially if they have an interest in, and knowledge of the subject matter emphasized by the museum.

Museum Attendants are sometimes hired from the membership of the museum's volunteer organization or governing body, as such persons have demonstrated their interest in the establishment and are knowledgeable about both operating policies and collection objects.

College students majoring in subjects compatible with the museum's emphasis are frequently considered for part-time jobs as Museum Attendants.

HELPFUL PERSONAL CHARACTERISTICS

Museum Attendants should be interested in the museum's collections to the extent that they feel a responsibility for their safekeeping and a need to learn about their origins and significance.

Because, in most cases, Museum Attendants are the only persons employed by the institution, they must be conscientious about performing their assigned duties, and self-assured enough to take necessary action to reprimand visitors, arrange for repairs to the premises, and maintain a good relationship with members of the governing body.

As the principal representative of the institution, the Museum Attendant should have good verbal skills, a friendly attitude, and the ability to communicate enthusiasm, as well as information, to museum visitors.

PHYSICAL DEMANDS AND ENVIRONMENTAL CONDITIONS

This is usually light work, performed in pleasant surroundings which vary according to the size, type, and physical condition of the museum.

WHERE TO FIND THESE JOBS

Most Museum Attendants work in small community institutions with an emphasis on history or science. These are usually operated by nonprofit organizations, but may also be funded by municipalities.

OPPORTUNITIES FOR EMPLOYMENT AND PROMOTION

Employment opportunities vary according to the turnover in individual institutions. Opportunities are likely to be greater in museums that hire college students for part-time work than in those that hire local citizens, who may stay in these positions for many years.

Because of the increase in new, small, community-oriented museums in towns and cities all over the United States, there should be a number of openings for Museum Attendants in the years to come. Persons with some college background in an academic field related to the museum's emphasis, especially if they are also familiar with the community, should have the best chance of securing these jobs.

MUSEUM INTERN

OCCUPATIONAL STATEMENT

Performs curatorial, administrative, educational, conservation, or research duties in museum or similar institution, to assist professional staff in utilization of institution's collections and other resources, and to gain practical experience and knowledge to enhance personal qualifications for career.

EDUCATION, TRAINING, AND EXPERIENCE

Museum internships serve a twofold purpose: to provide practical, on-the-job training for aspiring museum professionals, and to augment the efforts of staff members in carrying out both normal operations and special projects.

Internships vary in duration from 3 months or so to 2 or 3 years. Educational requirements vary from minimum of 2 years of college with curriculum emphasis in a field related to the specialty of the institution offering the internship, to a bachelor's or master's degree in a designated subject.

Remuneration may be in the form of a stipend, a grant-in-aid, or a straight salary, and rarely approaches the amount paid to permanent staff members.

Training is given to interns by professional staff members, and is usually geared to the academic specialization of both. For instance, an intern's work assignment may be to research European paintings and prepare a catalog of the museum's holdings in this field; orientation and general supervision will be given by the Curator in charge of the institution's collection of these paintings. A zoo intern may be assigned to teach after-school classes about the habits of nocturnal animals, and will be supervised by the institution's Director, Education.

In most cases, there are no experience requirements for internships. However, occasionally, such appointments do require museum experience and are available to persons currently working for museums who wish to broaden their employment and training background.

HELPFUL PERSONAL CHARACTERISTICS

Because of the variety of academic backgrounds required for internships offered by different institutions, it is impossible to generalize about all of the personal characteristics this job requires.

However, all persons interested in internships should be devoted to their chosen field, extremely serious about establishing themselves in careers in a museum or similar institution, and conscientious in their work habits.

Most internships involve research of one sort or another, requiring workers to have organizational and clerical abilities, as well as intellectual curiosity and logical thought processes.

Many internships are awarded on the basis of high academic achievement. Candidates for these positions should realize that, although the measure of learning is not always indicated by marks received, high marks may be the determining factor in hiring consideration to the institutions granting internships.

PHYSICAL DEMANDS AND ENVIRONMENTAL CONDITIONS

These vary according to the type of institution and the area of concentration, but should never include heavy physical activity or exposure to unpleasant or hazardous conditions.

WHERE TO FIND THESE JOBS

Internships are offered by art, history, science, multi-discipline, and specialty museums, as well as by zoos, botanical gardens, planetariums, and similar institutions. Most are with large establishments located in metropolitan areas, but smaller institutions throughout the country offer internships from time to time.

OPPORTUNITIES FOR EMPLOYMENT AND PROMOTION

Information about internships offered regularly may be found in the American Association of Museums' publication, Museum Training Courses in the United States. Data about internships which are not part of an institution's year-to-year operations may be obtained by writing to the American Association of Museums, or to the National Foundation for the Arts and the Humanities, the National Science Foundation, the Association for State and Local History, and other organizations which represent cultural institutions or provide funds for internship.

Colleges and universities that offer museum-oriented courses or that have working affiliations with specific museums of similar institutions may also provide this information, as will some public libraries.

Chances for employment as an intern depend too much on the academic achievement and specialization of applicants, the policies and priorities of institutions, and the ratio of available positions to candidates, for any valid statement to be made.

Persons hired as interns have excellent opportunities for advancement into full-time careers as museum professionals with the sponsoring institution or one with similar specialization.

MUSEUM TECHNICIAN

OCCUPATIONAL STATEMENT

Prepares specimens for museum collections and exhibits: Cleans rock matrix from fossil specimens using electric drills, awls, dental tools, chisels, and mallets. Brushes preservatives, such as plaster, resin, hardeners, and shellac on specimens. Molds and restores skeletal parts of fossil animals, using modeling clays and special molding and casting techniques. Constructs skeletal mounts of fossil animals, using tools such as drill presses, pipe threaders, welding and soldering apparatus, and carpenter's tools. Constructs duplicate specimens, using plaster, glue, latex, and plastiflex-molding techniques. Reassembles fragmented artifacts, and fabricates substitute pieces. Maintains museum files. Cleans, catalogs, labels, and stores specimens. May install, arrange, and exhibit materials.

EDUCATION, TRAINING, AND EXPERIENCE

Hiring requirements for these jobs vary, from graduation from high school to a year or two of college. High school graduates wishing to enter the field should have some shop courses and, preferably, courses in biology, zoology, and art. Persons with college training should have taken courses such as museum laboratory methods or museum exhibit techniques. Several universities offer programs, varying in length from a few months to 2 years, leading to acquisition of a certificate in this field. Certain junior colleges offer associate's degrees in a curriculum which includes preparation for this kind of work. At least one State museum sponsors a technician training program in cooperation with area high schools. The Occupational Statement above describes tasks of the job as they might exist in a small to medium-sized science museum with emphasis on anthropology, archeology, or one of the other social sciences. Museum Technicians employed elsewhere would perform other duties in addition to those described: fabrication of dioramas, refurbishment of preserved animals, birds, or reptiles, for instance, or even certain duties described here in the definitions for conservator, artifacts or Herbarium Worker. In none except the smallest museums, would Museum Technicians be responsible for maintaining files, cataloging or storing specimens, or installing exhibits. Differences in the duties included in the job in various establishments make it impossible to generalize about the hiring requirements for all positions of this type.

HELPFUL PERSONAL CHARACTERISTICS

Museum Technicians should be interested in, and capable of, working with their hands and using various tools and techniques to prepare or repair various artifacts for exhibit, and to construct or mold replicas of museum specimens, or fabricate dioramas.

They should be willing and able to take instruction from experienced workers, and also have the patience and pride necessary to work carefully and precisely on their assignments.

PHYSICAL DEMANDS AND ENVIRONMENTAL CONDITIONS

This is light work, usually performed in well-lit, climate-controlled indoor surroundings. Excellent eyesight is necessary, since near acuity, depth perception, and accommodation are required almost constantly. Manual and finger dexterity are also important in all of the work activities.

WHERE TO FIND THESE JOBS

Most Museum Technicians work in history or science museums operated by nonprofit organizations, as well as by Federal, State, and local government agencies. These are located in all parts of the country, in both metropolitan areas and smaller communities.

OPPORTUNITIES FOR EMPLOYMENT AND PROMOTION

Almost all museums would employ more technicians if funds were available. As increased financial support from both government and private sources is received, employment opportunities should be good for persons with training in this work. Some government-subsidized technician positions should be available through CETA or Work/Study programs for persons who meet the qualifications.

Museum-technicians can advance to jobs as exhibition specialists or, with additional training, positions in museum conservation work.

Federal civil service titles for entry jobs such as these are Museum Aid, GS 2/3, and museum technician, GS-4. They call for specialization in anthropology, geology, history, or other fields, and assignments are made on the basis of collection needs. Information about hiring requirements and entrance examinations may be obtained from Federal Job Information offices or, for jobs with the National Park Service, from personnel at the Harpers Ferry Museum Service Center in West Virginia.

PARK AID

OCCUPATIONAL STATEMENT

Performs variety of supportive duties, as directed by Park Ranger or Park Superintendent, to assist in operation of State or national park, monument, historic site, or recreational area: Greets visitors at facility entrance and explains regulations. When stationed at park offering camping facilities, assigns campground or recreational vehicle sites and collects fees. Monitors campgrounds, cautions visitors against infractions of rules, and notifies ranger of problems. Replenishes firewood and assists park workers to maintain camping and recreational areas in clean and orderly conditions. When stationed at historic park, site, or monument, conducts tours of premises and answers visitors' questions. Operates projection and sound equipment or otherwise assists ranger in presentation of interpretive programs. Provides simple first-aid treatment to visitors injured on premises and assists persons with more serious injuries to obtain appropriate medical care. Assists park workers and others to carry out fire-fighting or conservation activities. When stationed at historic or archeological site, assists other workers in activities concerned with restoration of buildings and other facilities, or excavation and preservation of artifacts.

EDUCATION, TRAINING, AND EXPERIENCE

This job has recently been added to the National Park Service list of classifications. It is similar to other paraprofessional jobs in that its purpose is to provide assistance to professional workers (Park Rangers) as well as to increase opportunities for Park Service careers for men and women without college training.

Park Aids must be high school graduates, and it is helpful for job candidates to have some work experience in a park or similar facility. They must also pass a written civil service test. Applicants for a similar job, that of park technician, must have either 2 years of college or 2 years of park experience.

There are a number of alternate combinations of education, training, and experience that may permit applicants to take civil service tests for these jobs. Information about these may be obtained from any Federal lob Information office.

Many State park systems also have jobs of this type, with similar hiring requirements. Some of these cooperate with State universities to offer work/study programs for undergraduates planning careers in recreation, conservation, or park work.

HELPFUL PERSONAL CHARACTERISTICS

Park Aids should enjoy public contact work, and be able to express themselves well, and feel comfortable with all of the many and diverse people who use the park's facilities.

They should be willing and able to perform a variety of duties, switching from one to another kind of work as directed by supervisory personnel.

Because the duties of specific positions vary greatly according to job locations, other characteristics may be needed by some workers: numerical and clerical ability, by aids who collect fees and maintain records; manual skill and an interest in science, by those stationed at archeological sites; and the willingness to perform routine, policing duties, by workers assigned to keeping camping areas in clean and orderly condition.

PHYSICAL DEMANDS AND ENVIRONMENTAL CONDITIONS

Both strength and activity requirements vary according to duties and work site. Park Aids assigned to historic monuments or similar facilities perform very little heavy manual work, whereas those stationed at large outdoor parks with extensive recreational facilities may be constantly active, cleaning campsites and carrying heavy loads of firewood. Most of this is outdoor work, except for jobs in facilities consisting solely of one or more structures, without appreciable surrounding acreage.

WHERE TO FIND THESE JOBS

Park Aids and technicians work in cities, suburbs, rural and wilderness areas, wherever State or national parks, monuments, historic sites or recreational areas are found. Although we usually associate the Western States with the National Park System, the majority of the system's 265 natural, historical, and recreational sites are located east of the Mississippi.

OPPORTUNITIES FOR EMPLOYMENT AND PROMOTION

Park Aid, and sometimes park technician, is an entry classification (meaning that it is usually not available to persons already employed by the State or national park system). Opportunities fluctuate according to the needs of various facilities and decisions by the Park Service to expand the services and increase the number of workers at specific locations. Since workers often advance to other positions from that of Park Aid, there are likely to be more openings for these jobs than for many others.

There are also seasonal openings for Park Aids and technicians in both national and State parks. Persons interested in summer jobs with the National Park Service should apply at any NPS Regional Office between December 1 and January 15 to be eligible for consideration the following summer. Although most States do not specify deadlines for applications for summer work contacting the appropriate State agency (Park Board. Department of Conservation or Department of Recreation) as early as possible in the year is always advisable.

PARK RANGER

OCCUPATIONAL STATEMENT

Enforces laws, regulations, and policies in State or national parks: Registers vehicles and visitors, collects fees, and issues parking and use permits. Provides information pertaining to park use, safety requirements, and points of interest. Directs traffic, investigates accidents, and patrols area to prevent fires, vandalism, and theft. Cautions, evicts, or apprehends violators of laws and regulations. Directs or participates in first aid and rescue activities. Compiles park-use statistics, keeps records, and prepares reports for review by Park Superintendent. May supervise workers engaged in construction and maintenance of park facilities, staffing of concessions, presentation of tours, or performance of other activities related to interpretation of park's special features. May plan, develop, and conduct programs to inform public of historical, natural, or scientific features, utilizing audiovisual devices, presenting illustrated lectures, and planning and supervising installation of visitors' center or other indoor or outdoor exhibits. May be responsible for cataloging, labeling, and storing historically or scientifically significant properties in collection of facility. May perform research to secure information needed to document collection items and assist in interpretation of park's theme. May survey park to determine forest conditions and characteristics of other natural phenomena, participate in ecological and other natural science studies, or in archeological and other social science studies. May be designated according to theme of park as Park Ranger (historian), Park Ranger (naturalist), or Park Ranger (archeologist).

EDUCATION, TRAINING, AND EXPERIENCE

To qualify for Park Ranger positions with the National Park Service, applicants must have a bachelor's degree with a minimum of 24 semester hours in at least one of the following areas: park and recreational management; field-oriented natural science; history; archeology; sociology; business administration; or one of the behavioral sciences.

This particular academic background may not be necessary for individuals who have at least 3 years of park or conservation experience. The Federal Service entrance examination must be taken by all persons wishing to become Park Rangers. Vacancies are filled from the register of names of persons who have taken this test and who meet the educational, experience, and specialization requirements for particular positions. State Park Ranger hiring requirements are similar to those for Federal jobs.

HELPFUL PERSONAL CHARACTERISTICS

Park Rangers should enjoy dealing with people in their job duties, and have good verbal skills, since in most positions they do some supervisory work, give information to park or historic site visitors, and present programs to the public. When working in a facility with a historic, natural science, or other specific theme, they should also be interested in the particular area of learning involved.

Park Rangers should also have organizational skills and leadership qualities. They should have the potential to respond quickly and efficiently to the emergencies which may vary, according to the work site, from vandalism to natural catastrophes. Rangers must know what to do, and be able to do it quickly!

PHYSICAL DEMANDS AND ENVIRONMENTAL CONDITIONS

Work varies from light to medium, depending on job location and duties performed. In almost all jobs, excellent physical condition is required, and physical examinations are given for some jobs.

Working conditions vary according to the type and location of the facility, with Ranger duties in the wilderness park areas likely to require a good deal of outdoor work in rugged surroundings.

WHERE TO FIND THESE JOBS

Rangers work in State and national parks, historic sites, and other facilities all over the country. All 50 States have national parks or other sites operated by the National Park Service, extending geographically from Acadia National Park in Maine to Glacier Bay National Monument in Alaska; from Everglades National Park in Florida, to John Muir Historic Site in California, Hawaii and the Virgin Islands have three national parks each, and Puerto Rico has one. Every State also has other parks, historic sites, and monuments where rangers are employed. Urban, rural, suburban, and wilderness areas all have installations such as these.

OPPORTUNITIES FOR EMPLOYMENT AND PROMOTION

Although one can always take the Federal service entrance examination and express an interest in becoming a Park Ranger, opportunities for employment will vary according to the academic specialization of the applicant, the turnover in specific installations, and the availability of qualified workers who may be promoted to ranger positions from within the system. Persons interested in this kind of work should also be aware that, despite their preference to work in a particular installation, rangers are hired according to need, and there is only a small possibility that new employees will be assigned to the site they prefer.

Park Rangers may be promoted to Park Superintendent jobs.

Opportunities for employment and advancement within the various States vary too much for any generalization to be made.

Some persons have the mistaken idea that Park Rangers and forest rangers are the same. The job of Park Ranger as described in this material, is found with the National Park Service, part of the Department of the Interior. Forest rangers, who are assigned to the Nation's forest land resources, work for the Department of Agriculture, in the National Forest Service, and are concerned, primarily, with conservation. These jobs are not covered in this book.

PARK SUPERINTENDENT

OCCUPATIONAL STATEMENT

Coordinates activities of Park Ranger and other workers engaged in development, protection, utilization, and interpretation of national, State, or regional park, recreational area, or historic site: Tours areas to assess development possibilities and determine maintenance needs. Prepares estimates of costs to plan and provide or improve fish and wildlife protection, recreation, expansion of facilities, and visitor safety. Selects, trains, and supervises Park Rangers. Directs workers engaged in rescue activities and fire suppression in park area. Investigates accidents, vandalism, theft, poaching and other violations, and presents evidence before court or designated legal authority. Answers letters of inquiry and addresses visitors and civic organizations to inform public of regulations and available facilities and to point out historical and scenic features of park. Prepares reports of area activities. May maintain records of attendance, permits issued, and monies received. May cooperate with administrators of other facilities to inaugurate, conduct, and report on research projects associated with historic or natural features of site.

EDUCATION, TRAINING, AND EXPERIENCE

All of these jobs are in Federal or State civil service systems, or equivalently structured State park service systems, where a combination of various education and experience requirements are needed as prerequisites for taking merit examinations. Preferred educational background is a bachelor's degree in park and recreation management, or, in positions at historically or scientifically significant locations, both management and appropriate history or natural science courses. Three or more years of experience in subordinate park management position are also required. Because the number of employees at national parks ranges from 10 to 400, superintendents may be in charge of the total operation of a small installation with limited acreage and perhaps one or two structures; or they may administer only one segment of an extremely large facility, with several superintendents reporting to an administrative superintendent. The combination of education and work experience mentioned above would be qualifying for workers to take the merit examination for this job. To be eligible for the position of administrative superintendent, extensive responsible service in a lower level capacity is required.

The hierarchies in State park systems are similar to those in the National Park Service, with satisfactory employment as Park Ranger usually required for these jobs. However, some States will place persons in superintendent positions without previous park experience if they have had administrative experience in similar installations, and/or if the park involved is extremely small.

HELPFUL PERSONAL CHARACTERISTICS

Park Superintendents are primarily administrators and should have the organizational skills, leadership ability, and business-oriented aptitudes needed to plan and direct the operation of the park. Because they are frequently required to represent the park, participating in workshops or presenting speeches or lectures, they should also be well versed in the important features of the facility, and possess poise and good communication skills.

PHYSICAL DEMANDS AND ENVIRONMENTAL CONDITIONS

This is light work which makes no unusual physical demands on the worker. Positions as superintendents are usually desk jobs, although some outdoor activity maybe required to tour and assess the condition of the premises.

WHERE TO FIND THESE JOBS

Park Superintendents work in large and small parks, historic sites, and similar facilities in urban, suburban, rural, and wilderness areas all over the country.

OPPORTUNITIES FOR EMPLOYMENT AND PROMOTION

Employment opportunities for Park Superintendents are limited by the amount of turnover in these positions in specific parks. There is little opportunity for persons from outside the State or Federal park system to become superintendents, as promotion to the posts is usually made from within.

Superintendents in large organizations may be promoted to the post of administrative superintendent. Those in small parks or historic sites may be appointed to similar posts in larger facilities. Such appointments usually entail a change in wage classification, although the job title remains the same.

PLANETARIUM TECHNICIAN

OCCUPATIONAL STATEMENT

Installs, modifies, operates, and maintains equipment used in presentation of planetarium classes or sky shows: Consults with personnel planning classes and shows to determine feasibility of achieving effects, modifications in equipment necessary to create desired effects, and additional equipment or properties to be incorporated into technical equipment layout. Following directions in script or lecture outlines, modifies theater projectors and other electro-optic equipment, console controls, and auxiliary instruments to adjust equipment capabilities for producing desired visual effects, basing modifications on knowledge of equipment capabilities and using handtools, precision instruments, and circuitry diagrams. Selects tapes of musical compositions from planetarium files and records portions of each, as designated in script, to produce tape recording with components of musical background in proper sequence. Modifies sound system to permit synchronization of recorded commentary and background music with visual presentation. Installs special effect properties, such as models of space ships or slides showing ancient interpretations of constellations, in designated positions in dome of theater, using handtools to secure properties to control wires or machinery to facilitate manipulation of properties according to script or lecture outline. Operates electro-optic, audio, and auxiliary equipment to present sky show or to complement presentation of class lectures. Maintains and makes minor repairs to equipment, using handtools and precision calibrating and testing instruments, applying knowledge of electronic circuitry and electro-optics, and following manufacturer's maintenance instructions and diagrams. May also construct and install permanent or temporary displays, incorporating electromechanical or electronic components, in planetarium's exhibit area.

EDUCATION, TRAINING, AND EXPERIENCE

Planetarium Technicians must have pre-employment training in the techniques involved in electrical and electronic wiring, and in the adaptation and operation of electromechanical, electro-optic, and electronic equipment. This may have been acquired in high school or technical school courses, or in a junior college. An associate's degree in electronic technology would provide acceptable background, especially if courses in the associated disciplines were included in the curriculum. In most planetariums, these workers must also have had previous work experience in which this training was utilized, and should be knowledgeable about the concepts and principles of optics, instrumentation, and sound projection. Depending on the number of persons employed by a planetarium, there may be from one to five technicians assigned to these duties. When only one is employed, his capabilities and overall knowledge must be broad enough that he can perform all duties listed; when several are employed, each may have a specialty, with one supervising technician planning and coordinating the individual work assignments to achieve the desired results. Even in institutions that employ several persons in this job, it is preferred that all technicians have a basic knowledge of all of the techniques required; they can then substitute for other workers if necessary, and also be able to devise or adapt the equipment they are most familiar with to produce the desired effects when operating it in coordination with other equipment.

HELPFUL PERSONAL CHARACTERISTICS

Planetarium Technicians should have an aptitude for, and an interest in, scientific and technical work. As the formal education required to develop the knowledge and understanding of the principles involved includes courses in higher mathematics, physics, and similar subjects, they must have good reading comprehension, and the mental ability to grasp highly complex information, as well as to translate it into practical applications.

They must also be able to work skillfully with their hands and fingers to position and fasten wires and other components accurately, to calibrate equipment controls, and to use precision instruments properly.

Numerical, spatial, and form perception are needed to read blueprints and diagrams, visualize constructions, and perform modification and repair work.

PHYSICAL DEMANDS AND ENVIRONMENTAL CONDITIONS

The duties associated with this kind of work have light to medium strength requirements. Skill in the use of hands and fingers is essential, as is excellent eyesight. Although most of the work is done in the planetarium workshop, quite possibly while seated or standing at a work table, stooping, crouching, crawling, reaching, and climbing may be required when the worker is installing, modifying, or repairing equipment. The ability to work easily in cramped quarters, as well as on scaffolding mounted high in the planetarium dome is important.

WHERE TO FIND THESE JOBS

Every planetarium employs people for this kind of work. Planetariums may be operated autonomously, may be part of a science center, or be included in the features making up a museum of science or technology. Most planetariums are located in metropolitan areas, although some associated with universities or public school systems may be found in smaller communities.

OPPORTUNITIES FOR EMPLOYMENT AND PROMOTION

There are usually openings for qualified Planetarium Technicians, either as full-time or part-time workers, because most persons with the required training and experience choose to work for industrial or service firms rather than in this particular work environment.

As with many other kinds of work in the museum field, opportunities for employment will increase if additional funds are made available to planetariums. Grants from the National Science Foundation, the Institute of Museum Services, and other supportive agencies should increase the capabilities of planetariums to hire Planetarium Technicians, as well as to offer salaries competitive with those paid for industrial or service work.

To find out about employment opportunities at specific planetariums, qualified persons should inquire at the personnel office of the establishment or, when the planetarium is operated by a city or other governmental entity, at the appropriate civil service headquarters.

PLANT BREEDER

OCCUPATIONAL STATEMENT

Plans and carries out breeding studies to develop and improve varieties of crops (or ornamental plants): Improves specific characteristics, such as yield, size, quality, maturity (color, appearance) and resistance to frost, drought, disease and insect pests in plants, using principles of genetics and knowledge of plant growth. Develops variety and selects most desirable plants for crossing. Breeds plants, using methods such as inbreeding, crossbreeding, backcrossing, outcrossing, mutating, or interspecific hybridization and selection. Selects progeny having desired characteristics, and continues selection and breeding process to obtain desired results.

EDUCATION, TRAINING, AND EXPERIENCE

This is professional work, almost always requiring an advanced degree in botany or horticulture, with specialization in plant genetics. Although simple plant breeding may be done by thousands of gardeners, both amateur and professional, the breeder whose job is described above is likely to be a full-time research worker whose efforts are devoted to producing improved strains of useful or ornamental plants. Jobs of this type in botanical gardens and similar institutions are usually obtained by people who have had experience as Research Associates, either while still in graduate school or immediately following graduation. As associates, they would have worked with other researchers, assisting them with their projects. They may have had the opportunity to develop and carry out research on their own with the goal of producing a hardier grass for lawns, or some giant-sized, especially beautiful, easy-to-cultivate rose. Persons interested in this kind of work should take as much science—biology, botany, and chemistry—as possible in high school to prepare for their college curriculum.

HELPFUL PERSONAL CHARACTERISTICS

Successful Plant Breeders should have extensive background knowledge of plant genetics and breeding methods, plus scientific curiosity, creative instincts, and the ability to persist in frequently lengthy processes to produce plants with the desired qualities. Those who are interested in working with plants, but like to see immediate results will not make good Plant Breeders. They must be able to work slowly and carefully, evaluate the results of research, and maintain detailed records of all steps involved in carrying out projects.

PHYSICAL DEMANDS AND ENVIRONMENTAL CONDITIONS

This is sedentary to light work performed in laboratories, controlled-temperature green houses, or outdoor test gardens or field locations. There are no unusual physical demands made on the worker, although dirt gardening is involved, and skill is required in the use of the hands and of such tools as knives, scrapers, and nutrient and pesticide applicators.

WHERE TO FIND THESE JOBS

Jobs as Plant Breeders are found at botanical gardens, arboretums, and certain natural history museums which have departments of botany. They may also be found in some large park systems whose management encourages innovation. Because plant breeding involves applied, practical research to produce desired qualities in useful or decorative plants, breeders may also be employed by companies that market or use cereal grasses or other grain products, or by large nurseries and seed companies. Federal Government employment of Plant Breeders may be with the Department of Agriculture or the Department of the Interior (U.S. Forest Service or National Park Service). Often, breeders employed by other institutions may be stationed on museum or garden premises and work with other professionals on joint projects.

OPPORTUNITIES FOR EMPLOYMENT AND PROMOTION

Employment opportunities in this field are limited by the amount of research funding available. Government grants by the National Science Foundation, the Department of Agriculture, or other agencies, may open more jobs for breeders. Also, some gardens and museums contract with private businesses to do research to develop crop plants with particular qualities. Very few breeders who have not had both distinguished academic backgrounds and experience or associations with universities, gardens, or museums will receive hiring consideration. Advancement opportunities vary; because of the intense concentration on research required by their duties, many Plant Breeders may not have the organizational and supervisory abilities needed to direct the activities of others, and such administrative work would be the most logical promotional step. If they do possess leadership qualities, they could advance to supervisory jobs in institutions with large research facilities, or to curatorial or exhibit planning work.

PLANT PROPAGATOR

OCCUPATIONAL STATEMENT

Propagates plants, such as orchids and rhododendrons, applying knowledge of environmental controls and plant culture (to maintain and develop stock of botanical garden, park, or institutional grounds): Confers with management (or supervisory) personnel to ascertain type and number of species to propagate and to develop and revise nutrient formulas and environmental-control specification. Selects materials according to type of plant; mixes growth media, and prepares containers, such as jars, pots, and trays. Initiates new plant growth, using methods such as the following: (I) Cuts leaves, stems, or rhizomes from parent plant and places' cuttings in growth media. (2) Bends, covers, or buries branches of parent plant in soil, securing branches with pegs or rocks. (3) Wounds stems of parent plant, using sharp knife, inserts pebble into wound and binds wound with moss, burlap, or raffia. (4) Plants meristem and seeds in growth media. (5) Breaks off or cuts apart and plants roots, crowns, and tubers from parent plant. Inspects growing area to ascertain temperature and humidity conditions, and regulates systems of heaters, fans, and sprayers to insure conformance to specifications. Gives transplanting and cultivation instructions to coworkers and monitors activities to assure adherence to established plant culture procedures. May graft or divide developing plants to promote altered growth characteristics. May log activities, maintain propagation records, and may compile periodic reports.

EDUCATION, TRAINING, AND EXPERIENCE

This is technical work, requiring either vocational training in horticulture at high school or junior college, or experience and on-the-job training as a grounds or greenhouse gardener. Since the passage of the Vocational Education Act in 1963, many high schools and junior colleges have offered classes in plant propagation, usually as part of a practical horticulture or commercial gardening curriculum. Such training could provide adequate preparation for jobs of this type, but most employers prefer to start recent graduates in less complex jobs and train them in the kinds of propagation techniques used at the specific establishment. Employers may also promote workers to these jobs without this formal training, but with satisfactory performance in gardening or greenhouse work.

HELPFUL PERSONAL CHARACTERISTICS

To do this job well, Plant Propagators should enjoy all aspects of dirt gardening. They should also like to work with their hands and be willing to follow the very precise procedures needed to propagate various kinds of plants. New Plant Propagators receive a good deal of direction in choosing the proper methods to use, but after a month or two in the job, they should be able to make these decisions themselves, on the basis of various plant properties. They should be willing to listen to more experienced workers, and also to read the gardening and other plant culture books that give directions for different types of propagation. Some of these include drawings or diagrams of propagation procedures; they should be able to translate these graphic directions into work activities. Because many of the techniques involved require cutting, bending, otherwise manipulating plant parts very precisely, propagators must work with care and precision.

As they will not always be the only persons caring for plants, they should be able to explain the techniques to other workers. This includes giving directions on the proper regulation of temperature and humidity controls in the greenhouse as well as the care of young plants.

PHYSICAL DEMANDS AND ENVIRONMENTAL CONDITIONS

This is light to medium work, but it requires quite a bit of physical agility, to bend, stoop, or squat while performing the various propagation duties. Manual and finger dexterity are needed to cut, bend, tie, and otherwise manipulate plant roots, buds, stalks or other parts during the propagation processes. The work is usually done in environment-controlled greenhouses, or out of doors in pleasant weather. There are no unpleasant or hazardous conditions associated with this job.

WHERE TO FIND THESE JOBS

Jobs as Plant Propagators may be found at arboretums and botanical gardens; city, State, national and other parks; institutions, such as zoos and museums, which maintain landscaped grounds, and historical communities, both restored and simulated. Plant Propagators may also be employed by landscape gardening firms, commercial nurseries, industrial and business establishments, and some amusement and recreational facilities. They are located in all areas of the country.

OPPORTUNITIES FOR EMPLOYMENT AND PROMOTION

This is a good field for people who like working with their hands in a nonindustrial setting. In many areas, there is a shortage of qualified applicants for this kind of work. Persons who have studied horticulture or commercial gardening in high school or junior college may be referred by school placement personnel to likely employers. However, recent graduates usually do not get Plant Propagator jobs immediately.

Those who are experienced in gardening or horticulture, either in a commercial nursery or other park or museum work, may find work in this field as a result of their earlier work history. Information about jobs of this kind with a park system may be obtained by consulting your State or local civil service authority. Federal jobs in gardening are available with the National Park Service and with certain other departments with public lands under their jurisdiction. Information about these can be obtained from the Federal Job Information office in your area.

Plant Propagators may advance to supervisory or managerial work in the same field.

RECREATION-FACILITY ATTENDANT

OCCUPATIONAL STATEMENT

Schedules use of recreation facilities, such as golf courses, tennis courts, and softball and sandlot diamonds, in accordance with private club or public park rules: Makes reservations for use of facilities by players. Settles disputes between groups or individual players regarding use of facilities. Coordinates use of facilities to prevent players from interfering with one another. May collect fees from players. May inform players of rules concerning dress, conduct, or equipment; may enforce rules or eject unruly player or unauthorized persons as necessary. May sell or rent golf and tennis balls, rackets, golf clubs, and other equipment. May render emergency first aid to injured or stricken players. May patrol facilities to detect damage and report damages to appropriate authority. May be designated according to facility tended, as golf course starter; tennis court attendant.

EDUCATION, TRAINING, AND EXPERIENCE

There are no stated hiring requirements for most of these jobs. Except in areas where both winter and summer recreational activities are available, the work is seasonal, and provides employment for a number of vacation job seekers. The majority of positions are with city parks, usually under civil service. However, unlike most local civil service employment, jobs as Recreation-Facility Attendants do not usually require the applicants to take merit examinations. Many jobs of this kind are obtained through summer jobs programs operated by communities, and the only requirements are that applicants be within a certain age group and meet the criteria for family income, area of residence, or other stated requirements.

Although previous experience in this kind of work is always desirable, it is not necessary. Employers usually train new employees for a week or two, to familiarize them with park policies and regulations. In the few places that offer full-time work of this kind, Recreation-Facility Attendants are usually required to be high school graduates with work experience (possibly acquired during summer employment) in this field.

Jobs in national and State parks having recreational facilities are usually obtained through application to the concessionaire who operates the facilities. Hiring requirements for jobs in these parks may vary from none at all to the specific attainment of a certain amount of formal education. Work experience is usually not required.

HELPFUL PERSONAL CHARACTERISTICS

These workers should enjoy meeting people, and should have good verbal skills and pleasant dispositions in order to explain rules and regulations, settle disputes firmly and diplomatically, and remain calm under circumstances that may be trying.

They should have good clerical and numerical skills, in order to make up schedules for the use of facilities, accurately record the names of users in the proper places, collect and record the receipt of fees, and maintain all records, not only for the periodic review of supervisory personnel, but also for use in settling disputes among the users of facilities.

The most important qualities employers look for in Recreation-Facility Attendants are dependability, honesty, and willingness to follow instructions. In small parks, responsibility for tending the tennis courts, golf course, or other facility, is often given to only one person. That person's failure to report to work, or sloppiness about maintaining records or collecting fees, could interfere with the efficient operation of the park.

PHYSICAL DEMANDS AND ENVIRONMENTAL CONDITIONS

This is usually light work, making no unusual physical demands on the worker. However, the requirements of individual jobs vary; some attendants may have to perform such duties as pulling rowboats to the dock and tying them to mooring rings, or policing a golf course for lost balls.

Although work is usually performed outdoors, shelter from the elements (in a booth or under a covered stand) is provided. When duties include selling equipment, more time is spent indoors in the shop, usually located next to the facility.

WHERE TO FIND THESE JOBS

Recreation-Facility Attendants work in State, national, local, and regional parks, certain zoos, botanical gardens, and other establishments that feature recreational facilities. They are located in metropolitan areas all over the country.

OPPORTUNITIES FOR EMPLOYMENT AND PROMOTION

There are always numerous opportunities for temporary work of this kind, especially for high school and college students. Information about jobs in city or regional parks may be obtained from the parks and recreation commissioner of the community in question, or from its personnel department. Information about jobs with national park concessionaires is available in the NPS publication, Seasonal Employment, which lists contacts for each of the parks. State park or conservation departments should be able to provide facts about available openings and application deadlines.

Opportunities for advancement to other positions from these jobs are limited.

REGISTRAR

OCCUPATIONAL STATEMENT

Registers visitors to public facilities, such as national or State parks, military bases, and monuments: Stops vehicles and pedestrians at gate and enters name, nationality, home address, license plate number of vehicle, and time of entrance and departure. Cautions visitors about fires, wild animals, travel hazards, and domestic pets, and informs them of laws and regulations pertaining to area. May issue informational leaflets. May collect fees and issue entry and fire permits. May give talks describing historical, natural, or scenic points of area.

May perform registration duties inside park or monument visitors' center rather than at entrance gate. May collect admission or parking fees from visitors entering park.

EDUCATION, TRAINING, AND EXPERIENCE

Information about education and experience requirements for jobs of this type in the National Park Service may be obtained from a Federal lob Information office. A variety of combinations of education and experience, none of which includes more than 2 years of college or 2 years of qualifying experience, are possible qualifications for taking the appropriate civil service tests. Hiring requirements for Registrar positions in State park systems are similar to those for National Park Service jobs. Specific information may be available from the various State civil service or park service commissions. Many of these jobs are seasonal, existing only during the summer months when tourist traffic is heavy. As usual for all seasonal employment, applications should be made no later than February 1. College students interested in summer work of this kind may receive extra consideration if their academic majors are in fields similar to those emphasized by the facilities where they wish to work: for example, archeology, geology, botany for many of the Western parks; U.S. history for many of the national monuments and historical parks.

This position does not exist in all national and State parks. Its duties are often performed by Park Rangers or Park Aids at facilities where visitor traffic is not heavy enough to warrant assigning one individual to the job.

HELPFUL PERSONAL CHARACTERISTICS

To enjoy this job, and to do it well, Registrars should be interested in meeting people, and be able to talk to them easily to explain park or monument regulations and answer their questions about special features of the area. Because records of visitors may provide important information for various authorities, Registrars should also have the clerical aptitude needed to be sure that all required information is on hand.

PHYSICAL DEMANDS AND ENVIRONMENTAL CONDITIONS

This is light work that makes few physical demands on the worker. In most positions, the worker is stationed in a gatehouse at the entrance to the park, and may perform all registration duties while seated inside. In parks with larger visitor center facilities, Registrars may also have the benefit of air-conditioned quarters. In time of emergencies or personnel shortage, Registrars may be required to perform other, more strenuous duties to assist in park operations.

WHERE TO FIND THESE JOBS

Gatehouse-located Registrars are most likely to work in State or national parks with large acreage and camping or hiking facilities. Jobs located in indoor visitor centers are likely to be at smaller historical or natural parks or monuments.

OPPORTUNITIES FOR EMPLOYMENT AND PROMOTION

Openings for this kind of job are determined by the stated needs of park superintendents and their evaluation by State or national civil service personnel. As the public use of State and national parks continues to grow, there may be an increasing need for Registrars for all types of facilities.

REGISTRAR, MUSEUM

OCCUPATIONAL STATEMENT

Maintains records of accession, condition, and location of objects in museum collection, and oversees movement, packing, and shipping of objects to conform to insurance regulations: Observes unpacking of objects acquired by museum through gift, purchase, or loan, to determine that damage or deterioration to objects has not occurred. Registers and assigns accession and/or catalog numbers to all objects in collection, according to established registration system. Composes concise descriptions of objects, basing composition on personal knowledge and information received from Curator, and recording descriptions on file cards and in collection catalog. Oversees handling, packing, movement, and inspection of all objects entering or leaving establishment, including traveling exhibits, and confers with other personnel to develop and initiate most practical methods of packing and shipping fragile or valuable objects. Maintains records of storage, exhibit, and loan locations of all objects in collection, for use of establishment personnel, insurance representatives, or other persons utilizing facilities. Prepares acquisition reports for review of curatorial and administrative staff. Periodically reviews and evaluates registration and catalog system to maintain applicability, consistency, and operation. Recommends changes in record-keeping procedures to achieve maximum accessibility to, and efficient retrieval of, collection objects. May arrange for insurance on objects on loan or special exhibition, or recommend appropriate insurance coverage on parts or entire collection. May photograph or direct photography of all new acquisitions, to provide visual documentation. May maintain collection records and oversee movement and handling of plants in botanical garden, and be known as plant registrar; may maintain inventory of animals owned by zoo and be designated animal registrar.

EDUCATION, TRAINING AND EXPERIENCE

Most Registrars have been employed in some other capacity in museum work prior to assuming these jobs. However, some recent graduates, with degrees in museology and courses in subjects appropriate to the emphasis of the institution, may be hired as Registrars, especially if they have served internships during which they learned registration techniques. Some familiarity with objects of the type owned by the institution is necessary, in order for Registrars to prepare accurate descriptions for catalogs and files, and to recognize evidence of damage to objects during shipment or movement. This knowledge could be obtained either through formal education or work experience. In some small history, science, or specialty museums, high school graduates may be hired to assist Registrars, and after lengthy experience, be promoted to these positions without college background.

HELPFUL PERSONAL CHARACTERISTICS

Registrars must have excellent clerical aptitude to follow the precise registration procedures used by the establishment. They also need good verbal ability to write clear and concise descriptions of objects, stating important facts and omitting unnecessary information.

These workers also need good business sense to understand insurance terminology and procedures, to recommend the most appropriate insurance coverage, and to be sure that financial and inventory records are kept in order.

Although most Registrars do not directly supervise workers engaged in moving or packing objects, they should have enough administrative ability to impress on persons responsible for these functions the need to follow methods to insure the preservation and safety of items concerned.

PHYSICAL DEMANDS AND ENVIRONMENTAL CONDITIONS

This is sedentary to light work, usually performed in pleasant indoor surroundings. It involves no hazards or unpleasant environmental conditions.

WHERE TO FIND THESE JOBS

Most medium to large-size museums employ Registrars to maintain collection records, as do a number of zoos and botanical gardens. In many smaller establishments, registration duties may be a part of curatorial or administrative positions. Some of the larger national and State parks may have Registrars on their staffs; however, most federally employed registration workers are in the Office of the Registrar at the National Park System's Division of Museum Services, and many State park systems also centralize the registration of objects.

OPPORTUNITIES FOR EMPLOYMENT AND PROMOTION

Because most establishments employ only one Registrar, there is less opportunity for employment in this capacity than in many other museum jobs. Chances for new workers to enter registration work are limited to openings occurring in already existing positions or to the creation of these positions in other establishments. Opportunities are greatest for persons with appropriate educational background and some experience in museum work.

There is little opportunity for advancement from this job to other positions in the same institution.

RESEARCH ASSOCIATE

OCCUPATIONAL STATEMENT

Plans, organizes, and conducts research in scientific, cultural, historical, or artistic field for use in own work or in project of sponsoring institution: Develops plans for projects, or studies guidelines for project prepared by Curator or other professional staff member, to outline research procedures to be followed. Plans schedule, according to variety of methods to be used, availability and quantity of resources, and number of subordinate personnel assigned to participate in project. Conducts research, utilizing institution's library, archives, and collections, and other appropriate sources of information, to collect, record, analyze, and evaluate facts. Discusses findings with other personnel to evaluate validity of findings. Prepares reports of completed projects for publication in technical journals, presentation to agency requesting project, or for use in further applied or theoretical research activities.

EDUCATION, TRAINING AND EXPERIENCE

With few exceptions, Research Associates have completed academic requirements for doctorates and are seeking opportunities to use and prove their scholastic achievements. These workers may be employed and paid by the institution, commercial enterprise, or government agency which subsidizes the cost of the project. Research projects may last for several months to 5 years or longer, and be conducted for such specific purposes as product development or ecological adaptation or, simply, to increase the body of knowledge about a certain period of history or scientific specialization. Both the purpose and the general field of research are determining factors in the hiring requirements for such posts.

HELPFUL PERSONAL CHARACTERISTICS

Research Associates must be able to apply their school acquired knowledges and techniques to solve problems or discover meaningful new information.

They must be capable of planning and organizing the steps needed to conduct a research project because they will receive little supervision from other persons; they also need clerical aptitude to record every procedure followed during the course of the project, and organizational and verbal abilities to prepare project reports.

As most of these workers have probably had 8 years or so of post-high school education, they have already demonstrated their interest in learning and their ability to concentrate on a particular kind of science, or period of history; they have been doing research for a number of years, beginning possibly with term papers during high school. To succeed as Research Associates, they simply need to continue to practice the good work habits that helped them to reach their chosen academic goals.

PHYSICAL DEMANDS AND ENVIRONMENTAL CONDITIONS

This is usually sedentary or light work, but actual physical requirements vary according to the type of research and the work location. Some work may be performed entirely in a library or laboratory setting, where little physical energy is required; other positions may include numerous field trips, with strenuous physical activity and exposure to hazards or unpleasant climatic conditions.

WHERE TO FIND THESE JOBS

Research Associates work at museums, zoos, botanical gardens, and other institutions. Most institutions are medium to large and many are associated with universities or colleges.

OPPORTUNITIES FOR EMPLOYMENT AND PROMOTION

At times, various institutions advertise for Research Associates, either in trade publications, or by sending announcements of openings to the graduate schools of colleges and universities. Other Research Associates are hired after presenting proposals for projects to institutions, together with their rationale and possible sources of funding. Numerous government agencies and nonprofit foundations supply funds for various research projects, through grants to both individuals and institutions. Of course, the applicant (whether would-be Research Associate or institution) must provide information to document the value of the project, as well as the capability of the person(s) assigned to it.

There is no way of predicting how many openings for Research Associates will occur in any given year as the needs of various institutions and the monies available fluctuate considerably.

Persons interested in this kind of work would contact the dean of their graduate school to find out about announcements or approach the appropriate staff members of other institutions to discuss possibilities of participating projects.

Research Associates may accept permanent, professional full-time positions at establishments where projects were conducted, or may receive special employment consideration from similar establishments as a result of this experience.

RESTORER, CERAMIC

OCCUPATIONAL STATEMENT

Cleans, preserves, restores, and repairs objects made of glass, porcelain, china, fired clay, and other ceramic materials: Cleans excavated objects by coating objects with surface-active agents to loosen adhering mud or clay and by washing with clear water. Places cleaned objects in dilute hydrochloric acid or other solution to remove remaining deposits of lime or chalk, basing choice of solvent on knowledge of physical and chemical structure of objects and destructive qualities of solvents. Cleans glass, porcelain, or similar objects by such methods as soaking objects in lukewarm water with ammonia added, wiping gilded or enamelled objects with solvent-saturated swab, or rubbing objects with paste cleanser. Removes stains from objects by rubbing with jeweler's rough or other mild abrasive, soaking in distilled water with appropriate bleach or solvent added, or applying paste or liquid solvent, such as magnesium silicate or acetone, basing choice of method and material on age, condition, and chemical structure of objects. Recommends appropriate preservation measures, such as control of temperature, humidity, and exposure to light, to curatorial and building maintenance staff, to prevent damage or deterioration of objects. Increases durability of ancient earthenware by impregnating surfaces with diluted synthetic lacquers to reduce porosity of material. Restores or simulates original appearance of objects by such methods as polishing surfaces to restore translucency, removing crackled glaze and applying soluble synthetic coating, grinding or cutting out chipped edges and repolishing surfaces, or applying matt paints, gold leaf, or other coating to object, basing methods and materials used on knowledge of original craft and condition of objects. Repairs broken or otherwise damaged objects by employing such techniques as bonding edges together with appropriate adhesive, inserting dowel pins in sections and cementing together, affixing adhesive coated strips to inner portions of broken objects, or replacing missing parts of objects by constructing wire frame of missing part, shaping plasticene or other material over frame, affixing modeled section to object with dowels or adhesive, and painting attached section to reproduce original appearance. Constructs replicas of archeological artifacts or historically significant ceramic ware, basing construction design on size, curvature, and thickness of excavated shards or pieces of objects available, and knowledge of techniques and designs characteristic of period. May train and supervise activities of museum aids. Museum Technicians, other workers, or volunteers engaged in restoration or minor repair of objects. May arrange for restoration or repair involving such techniques as glassblowing or reconstruction of particularly fragile pieces by specialists. May specialize in restoration and reconstruction of only archeological finds and be known as restorer, artifacts. May specialize in conservation and restoration of objects made of particular material and be known as conservator, glass, or conservator, earthenware.

EDUCATION, TRAINING, AND EXPERIENCE

Like other experts in the field of conservation/restoration, the Ceramic Restorer must have both formal education in appropriate subjects and hands-on training in appropriate methods. Undergraduate courses in art history, archeology, physics, chemistry, and ceramic engineering would provide background knowledge (acquired through workshops, seminars, graduate studies, or internships) needed for training in the practical application of various conservation, restoration, and repair techniques. Although it may be possible for persons without college degrees to get into this kind of work through on-the-job training, it is extremely rare. The objects involved are not only fragile, but often also irreplaceable, and employers are unlikely to entrust their care or restoration to anyone but fully competent, knowledgeable, and skillful workers.

HELPFUL PERSONAL CHARACTERISTICS

Ceramic Restorers must be able to understand and apply a large variety of scientific, historical, and artistic information. This means that would-be restorers must possess intelligence enough to benefit from college courses in the arts, sciences, and humanities. They should also have scientific curiosity, good clerical skills, and organizational ability to plan and carry out studies to verify the practicality of existing restoration techniques or to develop new ones. This kind of restoration also demands excellent finger dexterity and motor coordination to do the painstaking grinding, drilling, painting, and fitting of frequently minute fragments or objects. The Ceramic Restorer must be able to work slowly and deliberately, taking the utmost care to prevent damage or destruction of the valuable, sometimes priceless, objects worked with.

PHYSICAL DEMANDS AND ENVIRONMENTAL CONDITIONS

This is light work which requires excellent eyesight and manual skills but little other physical activity. It is usually performed in well-lit, climate-controlled laboratories or workrooms. Ceramic Restorers may accompany archeological expeditions and do some investigative, cleaning, and preservative work at the campsite, under conditions that may vary from primitive to comfortable, and that may be thousands of miles from home.

WHERE TO FIND THESE JOBS

Ceramic Restorers may work for science, history, art, multi-discipline, and specialty museums; for historical or ethnic community museums; for the Federal Government; or for restoration laboratories, both commercial and nonprofit.

OPPORTUNITIES FOR EMPLOYMENT AND PROMOTION

Properly trained Ceramic Restorers should have little trouble finding employment. Although a relatively small number of establishments employ workers in this capacity, there are usually even fewer well-trained applicants for jobs. Ceramic Restorers can become Art Conservators or heads of restoration laboratories, if they are familiar with preservation and conservation of other objects.

RESTORER, LACE AND TEXTILES

OCCUPATIONAL STATEMENT

Restores, repairs, and preserves textiles, lace, and fabricated textile items such as costumes, hand-woven coverlets, needlework samplers, or canvas tents, using methods and equipment appropriate to age, fiber structure, and construction of items: Cleans textile sample or item, using dry or wet cleaning technique to remove soil, stains, grease, and foreign matter, and choosing method and solvent appropriate to age, condition, and fabric. Dries wet-cleaned items under temperature-controlled conditions, supporting fragile items on frames to prevent disintegration or other damage. Restores fabric to original appearance or texture by applying textile paints or dyes, varnish, or other coating to textile sample or item, using care to preserve or restore original grain, texture, and color of material. Repairs worn, torn, decayed, or otherwise damaged textile samples or fabricated items by reweaving, handstitching, applying adhesive, mounting item on new cloth for reinforcement, or following other procedures. Develops new cleaning and repairing methods when available methods are inadequate or tend to harm materials. Advises curatorial, display, and maintenance personnel on environmental conditions, lighting, display, and storage methods required to preserve textile samples and items. May assign duties to and supervise activities of conservation technicians, museum aids, and Museum Technicians engaged in restoring or repairing textiles, lace, or fabric Items.

Many of these jobs are with the Federal Government. Incumbents usually have advanced though the ranks, after starting their careers as museum aids or Museum Technicians.

Textile restorers may advance to the position of conservator or administrator of a restoration laboratory if they had training in the conservation and restoration of other items and materials in addition to textiles.

EDUCATION, TRAINING, AND EXPERIENCE

Textile Restorers may learn their craft through formal education in conservation methods, or on-the-job training acquired as museum aids or Museum or conservation Technicians. The most likely formal education background would be completion of 4 years of college with a degree in history, art history, archeology, or anthropology plus graduate training in conservation and restoration of various kinds of textiles and fibers. Within this broad restoration area, Restorers may specialize in one or another kind of textile or fabric item. Some may concentrate on the restoration of ancient tapestries; some on reweaving of American Indian blankets and clothing; still others may become expert in the restoration of lace or of the costumes of a certain historical era. Expertise in each of these specialties may be gained through learning and working under an acknowledged expert in the field or by concentrating on a particular aspect of textile restoration during graduate training or internship.

HELPFUL PERSONAL CHARACTERISTICS

Like other workers in the area of conservation, the Textile Restorer must have the characteristics of both craftsman and scholar. The scholar studies existing methods of restoring or preserving textiles or devises new ones based on knowledge of the chemical and physical properties of textiles, solvents, and preservatives. The craftsman painstakingly performs the handwork that duplicates that done by the original weaver, seamstress, or other worker, deftly applies paints or dyes to recapture the original color of an item, or performs other tasks to restore or preserve items or textile samples as nearly as possible in their original state.

Textile Restorers need patience, good eyesight, skill in the use of their hands, and the ability to comprehend and apply the various methods of preserving or restoring textiles and fabricated items of many kinds.

PHYSICAL DEMANDS AND ENVIRONMENTAL CONDITIONS

This is light to medium work that makes no unusual physical demands on the worker. Good eyesight, especially in the qualities of near acuity, depth perception, and color vision, is important both for examining items to be restored and for duplicating the handwork of the original craftsman. Manual and finger dexterity are important in all restoration activities.

The work is usually done in a well-lit, well-ventilated laboratory or studio. Solvents, dyes, paints, and preservatives may cause unpleasant or irritating odors or fumes, but most restorers quickly become accustomed to these.

WHERE TO FIND THESE JOBS

Textile and Lace Restorers work in many history, multi-discipline, textile, ethnic, and industrial museums, as well as in restored communities, non-profit and commercial restoration laboratories, and certain government facilities.

OPPORTUNITIES FOR EMPLOYMENT AND PROMOTION

Persons with good training in textile preservation and restoration usually have no difficulty finding jobs. The increased public interest in, and institutional emphasis on, customs of the past and of various ethnic groups, as well as crafts in general, have brought about an increased need for workers who can restore textiles and needlecraft items. A number of institutions would hire more persons for these jobs if funds were available. Some trainee positions, financed through grants to the institutions or through subsidized work-training plans, are available to both high school and college graduates.

RESTORER, PAPER AND PRINTS

OCCUPATIONAL STATEMENT

Cleans, preserves, restores, and repairs books, documents, maps, prints, photographs, and other paper objects of historic or artistic significance: Examines or tests objects to determine physical condition and chemical structure of paper, ink, paint, or other coating, in order to identify the problem and to plan the safest and most effective method of treating material. Cleans objects by such methods as sprinkling crumbled art gum or draft powder over surface and rotating soft cloth over cleaning agent to absorb soil (dry cleaning), immersing objects in circulating bath of water or appropriate mild chemical solution (wet cleaning), or applying appropriate solvent to remove rust, fly specks, mildew, or other stains, basing choice of method on knowledge of physical and chemical structure of objects and effects of various kinds of treatment. Preserves or directs preservation of objects by such methods as immersing papers in deacidification baths to remove acidity from papers and ink to prevent deterioration, sealing documents or other papers in cellulose cases and passing sealed objects through heated rollers to laminate them, spraying objects, storage containers, or areas with fungicides, insecticides, or pesticides, and controlling temperature, humidity, and exposure to natural and artificial light in areas where objects are displayed or stored. Restores objects to original appearance by such methods as immersing papers in mild bleach solution to brighten faded backgrounds, removing old varnish from such art works as engravings and mezzotints, or strengthening papers by resizing in bath of gelatin solution. Repairs objects by such methods as mending tears with adhesives and tissue; patching and filling worm holes, torn corners, or large tears by chamfering, inserting, affixing, and staining paper of similar weight and weave to simulate original appearance; or retouching stained, faded, or blurred watercolors, prints, or documents, using colors and strokes to reproduce those of original artist or writer. May assign duties to and supervise work of museum aids or Museum Technicians, other workers, or volunteers engaged in performing simpler cleaning, restoring, or preserving tasks. May be known, according to objects treated, as document restorer, book restorer, photograph restorer, or conservator, art on paper.

EDUCATION, TRAINING, AND EXPERIENCE

Like other restorers, those concerned with paper must be well schooled in both academic and technical subjects. A bachelor's degree in art, art history, or history is the usual background, although degrees in museology, museography, or library science could also provide helpful training. Courses in organic and inorganic chemistry, physics, and botany are needed to understand the composition of various kinds of paper, ink, and other media. Conservation techniques are acquired at workshops or seminars and in graduate programs available at several universities and other institutions. Training in the restoration of documents may be obtained at institutions having extensive archival collections; for training in the restoration and preservation of both still and moving pictures, restorers must participate in workshops provided by institutions specializing in the field of photography. Hands-on training and experience are obtained by working as a Museum Intern, Technician, or apprentice, under the supervision of a craftsman in one or more of the special areas of paper restoration.

HELPFUL PERSONAL CHARACTERISTICS

Paper Restorers should have manual dexterity and coordination, extreme patience, and the ability to pay attention to details. In addition, they must have the intelligence to benefit from extensive formal education, and to understand and apply a number of techniques concerned with repairing, revitalizing, and preserving objects made on paper, with inscriptions, printing, coatings, or dye made of other organic or synthetic components. Because of the variety of possibilities in the chemical and physical structure of the materials involved, ranging from layers of ancient wallpaper in an historic home, to old drawings done in pastels on clay-surfaced paper, or water-soaked diaries salvaged from sunken ships, and the particularly fragile quality of paper itself, Paper Restorers may have chosen the most challenging of all types of restoration. People in this field should be both pragmatic and inventive to evaluate the effectiveness of all possible treatments for the particular job at hand and to search for or devise new ways of restoring noteworthy objects to their original condition.

PHYSICAL DEMANDS AND ENVIRONMENTAL CONDITIONS

Most work of this kind is performed in comfortable, climate-controlled laboratory or studio quarters. Excellent eyesight and manual and finger dexterity are needed to recognize sometimes minute flaws in objects to be treated and to use brushes, drafting instruments, and other handtools in some of the processes. Generally, this is light work which makes no unusual physical demands on the worker.

WHERE TO FIND THESE JOBS

Paper Restorers work for historical societies, large libraries, an and history museums, certain government agencies, and institutions that have large archival collections, as well as for some specialty museums and nonprofit and commercial restoration laboratories.

OPPORTUNITIES FOR EMPLOYMENT AND PROMOTION

Of all of the restoration fields, paper restoring probably has the greatest potential for employment. This is so for several reasons: more objects worth saving are made of paper—photographs, documents, books, artwork—and paper uncared for is the least permanent of materials. Also, though it may seem that today's society may, eventually, be lost in a mountain of paper records, this same society treasures and wishes to retain the paper records of yesterday. Well-trained specialists in this field should have no trouble finding employment. The Federal

Government, especially, offers a number of opportunities for work in this field. Opportunities for advancement vary according to the qualifications of the worker and the policies of the institution.

RESTORER, PAINTINGS

OCCUPATIONAL STATEMENT

Restores damaged and faded paintings and preserves paintings, using techniques based on knowledge of art and art materials: Examines surface of painting, using magnifying device, and performs tests to determine factors, such as age, structure, pigment stability, and probable reaction to various cleaning agents and solvents. Removes painting from frame. Applies select solvents and cleaning agents and uses predetermined method to clean surface of painting and remove accretions, discolorations, and deteriorated varnish. Stretches new linen backing, applies paste material to back of painting, and laminates parts together, using laminating press. Dries laminated painting under controlled conditions to prevent shrinkage. Applies beeswax or other substance to damaged or faded areas where restoration is needed. Studies style, techniques, colors, textures, and materials used by artist to maintain consistency in reconstruction or retouching procedure. Reconstructs or retouches damaged areas and blends area into adjacent areas to restore surface of painting to original condition. Applies varnish or other preservative to surface of painting and dries under controlled conditions. May remove paint layer from backing and remount on canvas, wood, or metal support using pressure and special adhesives. May apply neutral color powder to damaged areas to restore areas. May advise curatorial, administrative, and maintenance personnel on atmospheric conditions and other factors to preserve paintings in display and storage areas.

EDUCATION, TRAINING, AND EXPERIENCE

This is professional work, requiring an advanced degree with special training in the conservation and restoration of oil paintings.

At this time, there are only a few institutions in the United States which offer such training, plus a handful more in Europe. The usual requisite for such graduate study is an undergraduate degree in art history or art, with a number of courses in science, especially chemistry and physics, included. Skill in oil painting is also helpful, although Painting Restorers must paint in the style of the work being restored rather than their own. After acquiring graduate training, Painting Restorers may serve as interns or as conservation technicians, becoming familiar with the problems of conservation and restoration, and acquiring the skill needed to work with vulnerable paintings.

HELPFUL PERSONAL CHARACTERISTICS

A Paintings Restorer must combine a knowledge of chemistry and physics with an extensive knowledge of artists' techniques and materials, art history, and a sensitivity to painting styles.

A controversy exists over whether an aspiring restorer should have an interest in art or in science. An equal interest in both seems best, as too much concentration on art may retard the development of innovative techniques and too much attention to science may emphasize theory and experimentation to the neglect of practical application.

Similarly, the successful restorer must be an excellent craftsman and a serious student in order to know what to do and be able to do it.

Patience is essential for these workers because they must work for long periods at tedious and precise tasks. Frequently, more time is spent restoring a painting than the artist originally took to paint it! The Paintings Restorer at a medium-sized art museum treated 19 paintings in I year, and this was considered to be a large number.

Few people will be able to tell whether a restorer has done a good job on a painting; these workers, therefore, must have personal integrity and inner conviction in order to use and be satisfied with nothing less then their maximum skills of restoration.

PHYSICAL DEMANDS AND ENVIRONMENTAL CONDITIONS

This is light to medium work, requiring strength varying with the size and position of the painting and the type of restoration necessary. Excellent eyesight, including near and far acuity, depth perception, accommodation, and color recognition, is necessary.

Painting Restorers may stand or sit when working or, when renovating large works, may climb ladders, walk on scaffolding, bend, kneel, crouch, or stoop.

Most work is done in the laboratory or studio of the institution, where temperature and humidity are controlled. There is frequent exposure to the odors of various chemicals, paints, varnish, and solvents. Painting Restorers, however, would have had ample time to adjust to these fumes earlier in their careers.

WHERE TO FIND THESE JOBS

Art museums, some multi-discipline museums, the Federal Government, nonprofit and commercial restoration laboratories all hire Painting Restorers.

OPPORTUNITIES FOR EMPLOYMENT AND PROMOTION

The well-qualified Paintings Restorer has little difficulty in finding work, either with an institution or a laboratory. This is painstaking, complex work, for which there are too few persons prepared. Painting Restorers may also freelance as self-employed experts, offering their services to the many institutions that do not have such workers on their staffs. They must have established reputations for excellence in the field, however, and usually must have had work experience in a museum or laboratory. Painting Restorers may become Art Conservators or, in some institutions, may take administrative posts if they are willing to forsake this technical work for the equally demanding tasks of the Director.

SALESPERSON, GENERAL MERCHANDISE

OCCUPATIONAL STATEMENT

Sells variety of commodities in sales establishment: Greets customer and ascertains make, type, and quality of merchandise desired. Displays merchandise, suggests selections that meet customer's needs, and emphasizes selling points of article, such as quality and utility. Prepares sales slip or sales contract. Receives payment or obtains credit authorization. Places new merchandise on display. May wrap merchandise for customer. May take inventory of stock. May requisition merchandise from stockroom. May demonstrate use of merchandise. May examine defective article returned by customer to determine if refund or replacement should be made.

EDUCATION, TRAINING, AND EXPERIENCE

There are no fixed hiring requirements for these jobs, but most employers require full-time workers to be high school graduates. Previous selling experience is helpful, but not necessary; on-the-job training, from I week to 2 weeks in length, is given to new workers by the Store Manager or an experienced salesperson. Seasonal positions are usually filled by high school or college students.

HELPFUL PERSONAL CHARACTERISTICS

Because this Occupational Statement covers positions in many different kinds of sales operations, there are a variety of personal characteristics that would be helpful. Salespersons who work in book or gift shops that carry merchandise associated with some of the institution's collection of objects must be knowledgeable about the subject matter in order to answer customer's questions and make viable suggestions. For those who work in snack bars or souvenir stands, this quality is not so important; however, these Salespersons must be able to keep calm and perform their work quickly and efficiently when serving throngs of adults and children, all wanting immediate attention.

Clerical and numerical aptitude are important for most of these jobs, as Salespersons must make change and maintain some records.

All Salespersons should be patient and courteous and really enjoy working with other people.

PHYSICAL DEMANDS AND ENVIRONMENTAL CONDITIONS

Strength requirements vary from light to medium, depending on the amount of traffic at the stand or in the shop, and the type of merchandise sold. Standing is constant in most positions, with frequent reaching and occasional bending and stooping required. There are no unusual physical demands made on workers, nor are they exposed to uncomfortable or dangerous environmental conditions.

WHERE TO FIND THESE JOBS

All but a few establishments of this kind operate gift shops, souvenir stands, and snack bars. Although a few museums staff their shops with volunteers, the vast majority hire people for these jobs. Most museums and similar institutions operate their own gift shops and souvenir stands; snack bars, restaurants, and other food-vending facilities are most likely to be operated by concessionaires who hire their own workers and remit a percentage of the profit to the institution. All food and gift stands in or adjacent to National Park Service facilities are operated by private companies and individuals.

OPPORTUNITIES FOR EMPLOYMENT AND PROMOTION

Because more and more institutions have stopped depending on volunteers to staff their retail facilities, opportunities for Salespersons are increasing. Hiring preference will be given to individuals who have some background knowledge about the institution's specialization, as well as to persons who may have worked in museum shops as volunteers. Information about the hiring requirements of individual institutions may be obtained at their personnel offices.

Persons interested in seasonal work should apply at the personnel office of the institution (or at the appropriate civil service office when the establishment is government operated) 5 or 6 months prior to the date that the facility will be opened. Information about seasonal sales work in the national parks may be obtained by writing for the National Park Service publication, Seasonal Employment.

Salespersons may advance to the job of Store Manager in most institutions.

SCHEDULER

OCCUPATIONAL STATEMENT

Makes reservations and accepts payment for group tours, classes, field trips, and other educational activities offered by museum, zoo, or similar establishments: Provides information regarding tours for school, civic, or other groups, suggests tours on institution calendar, and contacts group leaders prior to scheduled dates to confirm reservations. Provides information regarding classes, workshops, field trips, and other educational programs designed for such special groups as school or college students, teachers, or handicapped persons. Registers groups and individuals for participation in programs, enters registration information in department records, and contacts participants prior to program dates to confirm registration and provide preparatory information. Prepares lists of groups scheduled for tours and persons registered for other activities, for use of Director, Education. Collects and records receipt of fees for tours, classes, and other activities. Maintains records of participating groups, fees received, and other data related to educational programs, for use in preparation of department reports. May take reservations and sell advance tickets to exhibits, concerts, and other events sponsored by institution. May prepare periodic summaries of department activities for review by administrative personnel. May arrange for use of special equipment, or for support of volunteer organization, to facilitate presentation of special activities.

EDUCATION, TRAINING, AND EXPERIENCE

Employers usually require that Schedulers have at least a high school education and the ability to type. Because accuracy is more important than speed, clerical work experience is not essential, although, as for most other office work, applicants with previous related experience are likely to be given first consideration. In most places, new workers are given training to familiarize them with the institution's policies and activities before they begin actual job duties.

HELPFUL PERSONAL CHARACTERISTICS

Schedulers should have at least average clerical ability to record information accurately on a variety of forms and to maintain files in such a way that they, and other employees, can retrieve information quickly and easily. Because requests for information may come by mail or telephone, or from department visitors, Schedulers should be able to express themselves well, both orally and in writing, to provide clear and concise answers to questions about the programs. They should also really enjoy dealing with people at all levels and be able to maintain a pleasant, unruffled disposition even when their work is interrupted by phone calls or demanding visitors. Although this may seem to be routine clerical work, the Scheduler must be capable of performing a variety of tasks such as filing, typing, and scheduling, as the need for them arises, maintaining both efficiency and poise.

PHYSICAL DEMANDS AND ENVIRONMENTAL CONDITIONS

This is light work that makes no unusual physical demands on the worker. It is usually performed in a pleasant, climate-controlled office.

WHERE TO FIND THESE JOBS

People performing the duties of Scheduler work in all institutions that offer more than minimum educational and public service programs. In some small establishments, however, this work may be done by another clerical worker and does not exist as a separate job. In large museums with very extensive programs, several people may share the duties, with each being in charge of registration and scheduling for a particular kind of activity.

OPPORTUNITIES FOR EMPLOYMENT AND PROMOTION

These vary according to both the size and the operating policies of establishments. As more emphasis is placed on the education programs of museums and similar institutions, there should be more openings in this kind of work. Schedulers may advance to such jobs as Membership Secretary or volunteer coordinator with no additional education or training. Without some post-high school education, or a unique technical skill, it would be difficult to get into other professional or administrative museum work.

SECURITY CHIEF, MUSEUM

OCCUPATIONAL STATEMENT

Supervises and coordinates activities of guard force of museum, zoo, or similar institution: Assigns personnel to posts or patrol, according to size and nature of establishment and protection requirements. Interprets security rules and directs subordinates in enforcing compliance, such as issuance of security badges, photographing of employees, and safekeeping of forbidden articles carried by visitors. Responds to calls from subordinates to direct activities during fires, storms, riots, or other emergencies. Inspects or directs inspection of premises to test alarm systems, detect safety hazards, and to insure that safety rules are posted and enforced. Examines fire extinguishers and other equipment for serviceability. Reports irregularities and hazards to appropriate personnel. Selects and trains subordinates in protective procedures, first aid, fire safety, and other duties. Cooperates with police, fire, and civil defense authorities in handling problems affecting establishment.

EDUCATION, TRAINING, AND EXPERIENCE

A person may become the Security Chief of a museum or similar institution after several years' experience as a Guard in the same establishment or by entering the post directly from a similar job with the armed forces or a city police department. Specific educational requirements vary, but almost all establishments require that these workers have a minimum of a high school education. Knowledge of the premises to be guarded is necessary and may have been obtained during their tenures as Guards, by workers who have been promoted from within. Security Chiefs who are new to the institution, no matter what their background and general knowledge of procedures must have orientation training to acquaint them with the size and general features of the premises, and the location of various objects that require special protective measures.

HELPFUL PERSONAL CHARACTERISTICS

Security Chiefs must have organizational ability to plan and supervise the activities of Guards, to arrange their own schedules wisely, and to coordinate the function of the security division with those of other sections of the institutions. They should be good judges of people and able to get along well with others, in order to select qualified persons for Guard positions; train and monitor the work performance of subordinates; and work with administrators and representatives of the police department and other outside agencies to implement the security program of the institution. Security Chiefs must also be able to stay calm during crises and have the self-confidence and initiative to take charge of problem situations, such as fires, thefts, and other such occurrences, should they arise.

PHYSICAL DEMANDS AND ENVIRONMENTAL CONDITIONS

This is light work which, except in emergency situations, makes few physical demands on the workers.

WHERE TO FIND THESE JOBS

Security Chiefs work for medium to large institutions of all kinds. Smaller museums with security forces usually do not hire persons for supervisory positions in this field but assign the duties of supervising Guards to another employee. Museums and other institutions that engage the services of a commercial firm to provide Guards often employ their own Security Chiefs to train and supervise the activities of the workers assigned to these institutions.

OPPORTUNITIES FOR EMPLOYMENT AND PROMOTION

There are relatively few openings for these jobs for persons not already employed as Guards, although, with increasing security problems, more institutions may prefer to hire persons with supervisory experience in the armed forces or police work rather than to promote from within the organization.

Except in very large institutions that employ a number of persons in supervisory positions in the security field, there is no opportunity for advancement for Security Chiefs who stay with the same employer.

SUPERINTENDENT, HORTICULTURE

OCCUPATIONAL STATEMENT

Plans, coordinates, and directs activities concerned with breeding, growing, and displaying ornamental flowers, shrubs, and other plants in botanical garden, arboretum, park, or similar facility: Confers with administrative, technical, and maintenance staff members to plan operations most appropriate for maintenance of growing stock and the production of plants for display on grounds, installation in special exhibits, for sale to public, or for use in research projects. Discusses with administrative personnel plans for renovation or additions to facility and devises designs for floral exhibits to complement theme of new or renovated sections. Prepares scale drawings of outdoor or greenhouse exhibits for use of gardening staff members. Issues instructions to supervisory personnel in charge of growing, greenhouse, and display activities. Inspects greenhouse, hothouses, potting sheds, experimental growing areas, and other areas to determine need for repair and to observe activities of workers. Maintains inventory of propagation and growing equipment and supplies and orders additional materials as needed. Arranges purchase, sale, or exchange of plants with representatives of similar institutions. Confers with Plant Breeders and other research personnel to discuss development of new strains of plants and devise methods to exhibit, publicize, or market them. May represent establishment at civic or professional meetings. May participate in radio or television shows or prepare articles for newspapers to provide horticultural information to public.

EDUCATION, TRAINING, AND EXPERIENCE

This is professional administrative work, usually requiring a degree in horticulture or one of its specialties, plus work experience in both the practical application of horticultural principles and the use of these principles in research projects.

Because the Superintendent, Horticulture, must exercise overall supervision of work activities involved in growing plants, installing displays, and all other establishment functions, a working knowledge of the technical aspects of horticulture is critical. Usually, persons advance to these jobs from less responsible positions with the same, or a similar, institution. However, some small botanical gardens or park systems may hire these specialists without work experience, if their academic background has included the practical application of horticultural principles.

HELPFUL PERSONAL CHARACTERISTICS

This job is a good example of the kind of work for which both scientific and business interests are needed. Horticulturists must be interested in, and knowledgeable about all of the techniques involved in growing and maintaining a large variety of plants. In jobs such as these, however, their actual duties are administrative; they must be able to get along well with people at all levels of educational achievement, plan their own activities and those of others, and conduct the business of the institution efficiently.

Horticulturists should also have a certain amount of creativity to design attractive and appropriate displays.

PHYSICAL DEMANDS AND ENVIRONMENTAL CONDITIONS

This is light work, performed, for the most part, in an office environment. The Superintendent, Horticulture, tours the growing and display areas to inspect the premises and evaluate the work of others, but such activities are not strenuous.

WHERE TO FIND THESE JOBS

Superintendents, Horticulture, are employed by botanical gardens, aboretums, public parks of all kinds, and other institutions that have extensive grounds with floral displays.

OPPORTUNITIES FOR EMPLOYMENT AND PROMOTION

For persons not already employed in this field, opportunities for employment as Horticulture Superintendents are limited to the occasional openings that occur in smaller botanical gardens or park systems.

TAXIDERMIST

OCCUPATIONAL STATEMENT

Prepares, stuffs, and mounts skins of birds or animals in lifelike form: Removes skin from dead body with special knives, scissors, and pliers, taking care to preserve hair and feathers in natural state. Rubs preservative solutions into skin. Forms body foundations by building up on wire foundation with papier mache and adhesive tape, to give natural attitude and show form and muscles of specimen. Covers foundation with skin, using specified adhesive or modeling clay. Affixes eyes, teeth, and claws; dresses feathers and brushes fur to enhance lifelike appearance of specimen. May mount specimen in case with representations of natural surroundings. May make plaster cast of specimen to enhance physical details preparatory to making papier mache mold. May dress-out, preserve, or otherwise prepare animal carcasses for scientific or exhibition purposes.

EDUCATION, TRAINING, AND EXPERIENCE

There are no established hiring requirements for Taxidermists employed in these institutions other than they be able to perform the duties as described in the Occupational Statement. Training in taxidermy may be obtained on the job, as a helper or assistant in a commercial taxidermy studio where animals and birds are stuffed and mounted for sportsmen, collectors, or museums; as part of the curriculum graduate or undergraduate college courses in exhibit techniques (museography); or through participation in museum apprenticeship programs concerned with the collection and preparation of exhibits. The general education preceding any of these kinds of training should include courses in art, biology, and anatomy.

HELPFUL PERSONAL CHARACTERISTICS

Taxidermists should enjoy working with their hands, have good manual and finger dexterity, and have spatial and form perception to do the precision work involved in removing and mounting the skins of animals.

Taxidermists are craftsmen and artists because they can reproduce the physical appearance of animals, and also stylize it. However, they should have pride in their own workmanship which is shared by both artists and craftsmen and be able to work patiently and painstakingly, concentrating their entire attention on the task at hand.

121

PHYSICAL DEMANDS AND ENVIRONMENTAL CONDITIONS

This is light to medium work, usually performed in well-lit workshops or laboratories. Good eyesight, particularly the factors of near acuity, depth perception, and accommodation, is essential; as are manual and finger dexterity and coordination.

Many of the specimens to be mounted consist only of the frozen, salted, or otherwise preserved animal hides, since the actual skinning and removal of flesh and bones have been done at the point of capture. Hides and skins of imported animals have also been fumigated, to destroy fungus or insects, as required by the U.S. Department of Agriculture. Working with unskinned animals (which may be fresh, frozen, or preserved in salt at the time of delivery) require more work by the Taxidermists, since the animals must be skinned, the flesh, viscera, and bones disposed of, and the hide sprayed with preservative prior to mounting. Although one might suppose that unpleasant odors would characterize this work, persons in the field explain that if the animal has reached the point of decay causing odors, it is not a fit subject for taxidermy.

There may be some revulsion associated with skinning and discarding the carcasses of animals, but persons who wish to succeed as Taxidermists soon overcome any feelings of distaste.

WHERE TO FIND THESE JOBS

Most museum Taxidermists work for the larger science or natural history institutions located in metropolitan areas. In smaller museums, technicians may perform taxidermy work in addition to their other duties. Taxidermists also are employed in commercial studios, which may specialize in work for museums or may stuff and mount fish, birds, and other animals for the general public as well. There are a number of these studios in medium and large cities all over the country.

OPPORTUNITIES FOR EMPLOYMENT AND PROMOTION

Taxidermy is an extremely specialized skill, and persons who are trained in its techniques usually have no trouble finding employment. Owing to both cost and convenience factors, most museums would prefer to hire people to do this work, rather than use the services of commercial studios. When and if financial support of museums, either by the government or private sources increase, more opportunities for Taxidermists should be available.

Persons who have had training in other exhibit techniques as well as taxidermy will find it easier to obtain museum jobs than will those who are trained only in this skill.

Taxidermists in the museum field can be promoted to supervisory jobs in the construction and installation of exhibits.

TEACHER

OCCUPATIONAL STATEMENT

Teaches classes, presents lectures, conducts workshops, or participates in other activities to further educational program of museum, zoo, or similar institution: Confers with other education staff members to determine department goals, identify individual responsibilities, and plan course content and method of presentation. Prepares outline of materials to be covered in course, lecture series, workshop, or seminar, for approval by Director, Education. Selects and assembles materials, such as pieces of pottery or samples of plant life, to be used in teaching assignment and arranges for use of audiovisual equipment or other teaching aids. Under supervision of Director, Education, performs any combination of the following activities to carry out institution's educational program: Conducts classes for children in various scientific, history, or art subjects, using museum displays to augment standard teaching methods and adapting course content and complexity to ages and interests of students. Teaches adult classes in such subjects as art history, astronomy, or horticulture, using audiovisual aids, demonstration, or laboratory techniques appropriate to subject matter. Presents series of lectures on subjects related to institution's collections, often incorporating films or slides into presentation. Conducts seminars or workshops for school system teachers or laymen to demonstrate methods of using institution's facilities and collections to enhance school programs or to enrich other activities. Conducts workshops or field trips for students or community groups; plans and supervises activities associated with projects. Plans and presents vacation or weekend programs for elementary or preschool children, combining recreational activities with teaching methods geared to age groups. Conducts classes for academic credit in cooperation with area schools or universities. Teaches courses in museum work to participants in work/study programs. Works with adult leaders of youth groups, to assist youths to earn merit badges or fulfill other group requirements. Maintains records of attendance. Evaluates success of courses, basing evaluation on number and enthusiasm of persons participating, and recommends retaining or dropping course in future plans. When course is offered for academic credit, evaluates class members' performance, administers tests, and issues grades, in accordance with methods used by cooperating educational institution.

EDUCATION, TRAINING, AND EXPERIENCE

Employer's hiring requirements for these jobs vary greatly because of the great variety in educational programs sponsored by different institutions. Generally, a bachelor's degree in a subject related to the museum's emphasis is the minimum requirement. Experience in teaching that subject is desirable but often unnecessary. Teachers who specialize in lecturing must have expertise in their chosen fields, acquired either through formal study leading to an advanced degree, or through extensive work experience. In some institutions, individuals who conduct programs for elementary or preschool children may need only I or 2 years of college if they have had successful experience working with young children in other capacities. Some museum education staff members double as faculty members of a university or hold jobs in private industry.

HELPFUL PERSONAL CHARACTERISTICS

Most institutions consider the ability to communicate well with class members at least as important as familiarity with the subject matter being presented. Teachers should be enthusiastic about their subjects and able to transmit this enthusiasm to the children or adults participating in education programs.

Good organizational ability is needed to outline materials to be presented, to make arrangements for the use of appropriate audiovisual materials and other equipment, and to keep course records.

When conducting classes for credit in other educational facilities, Teachers should be willing to follow accepted format so that students are able to earn the specified academic credits.

Teachers who work with young children should be able to translate the scientific or historical facts presented into language their small charges will understand and to develop creative methods of presenting information.

PHYSICAL DEMANDS AND ENVIRONMENTAL CONDITIONS

This is usually light work, making no unusual physical demands on the worker. However, it does require both sustained speaking ability and energy in order to present lectures, conduct classes, and demonstrate various craft techniques. The work may be performed in a variety of settings. Some museums have special auditoriums or classroom sections, while others set aside exhibit galleries to be used as classrooms. Some classes may be conducted in greenhouses or animal compounds or at archeological sites. There has been a recent trend toward sending museum personnel into inner city areas, and some classes may be taught in community centers, schools, or other off-site locations.

WHERE TO FIND THESE JOBS

Almost every museum, zoo, and similar facility has an education program. The size of the education staff varies according to the size and the emphasis of the institution. Some large museums employ as many as 25 or 30 people as Teachers. In this kind of organization, Teachers are likely to specialize in presenting classes in only one subject to adult, youth, or children's groups, or to teach classes either for credit or for recreational purposes. Other institutions with less ambitious educational programs may employ only two or three Teachers who present many different kinds of classes.

OPPORTUNITIES FOR EMPLOYMENT AND PROMOTION

Teaching jobs in museums and similar institutions may be either full time or part time, permanent or temporary. Some Teachers may divide their time between museum work and jobs on college faculties or in industry. Because cultural institutions, generally, plan to expand their educational programs to serve better both school groups and their communities, opportunities for teaching jobs in this field should increase. Teachers may advance to positions as Directors, Education, in the same, or similar establishments.

TRANSPORTATION EQUIPMENT MAINTENANCE WORKER

OCCUPATIONAL STATEMENT

Performs any combination of following tasks to assist in reconstruction, renovation, refurbishment, or maintenance of transportation equipment such as automobiles, ships, aircraft, streetcars, or locomotives displayed by museums or similar institutions: As directed by supervisory personnel, repairs or replaces interior components of equipment, such as wooden panels, seat cushions, window molding, or dashboards, using hand and power tools and employing appropriate carpentry, metalworking, upholstering, or other techniques. Assists other workers in reconstruction or renovation of exterior structural sections and accessories by performing such duties as cutting lumber or sheet metal to designated size, installing components such as brake assemblies, rudders, or propellers, or welding together metal sections. Refurbishes equipment by performing such duties as cleaning surfaces with wire brushes or appropriate solvent, applying rustproofing agent to surfaces, vacuuming and dry-cleaning upholstered components, brushing or spraying paint, lacquer, or other coating on cleaned surfaces, or stenciling or painting lettering or designs on equipment or vehicles, to restore or simulate original appearance. Maintains appearance of displayed equipment by cleaning and polishing parts, using appropriate solvents, waxes, or other agents. Builds, repairs, and installs wooden steps, scaffolds, and walkways used to gain access to or permit improved view of exhibited equipment. May be designated according to specialty of institution, as antique auto museum maintenance worker, according to principal activity, as maintenance carpenter, or according to job location, as exhibit cleaner.

EDUCATION, TRAINING, AND EXPERIENCE

There are no specific hiring requirements for this kind of work which are applicable to all institutions. Transportation Maintenance Workers in most museums and similar institutions are not required to have had previous employment in structural work.

Although work on the maintenance and repair of transportation equipment would usually imply that some sort of experience on mechanical or electrical parts would be helpful, this is not the case with these jobs.

In most instances, the aircraft involved does not have to be flown, or the automobiles driven, or the ships piloted. Maintenance workers are concerned with helping to make these vehicles appear to be functional rather than to make them function.

Therefore, institutions that hire people for these jobs are usually willing to train them in the techniques used. High school shop courses in woodworking, metalworking, and other manual arts provide good background for this kind of work, as do hobbies that involve the use of hand and power tools to work wood or metal.

In some localities, hiring institutions cooperate with vocational high schools in work/study programs, through which students learn to apply their skills, receive wages, and also acquire experience helpful to securing full-time employment or being accepted into a craft or construction apprenticeship program. Most of these institutions employ skilled supervisory or craft workers, under whom the maintenance workers are trained.

HELPFUL PERSONAL CHARACTERISTICS

Persons doing this kind of work should enjoy working with their hands and have at least average dexterity to use the hand and power tools needed to fabricate, install, or repair the structural parts of the equipment involved, or to paint and decorate it attractively and authentically.

They should also be able to follow instructions of supervisory personnel and be willing to take the time to do careful and accurate work.

Although it is not an absolute job requirement, Transportation Equipment Maintenance Workers are most likely to succeed in their work if they develop an interest in the kind of equipment they are working on—how it was operated, what its uses were, and how it related to the customs of a particular period or locality. Such an interest will not only help them do a good job of reproducing the original appearance of the equipment but also advance to higher paying jobs involving research into restoration techniques concerned with other historically significant objects.

PHYSICAL DEMANDS AND ENVIRONMENTAL CONDITIONS

This is medium to heavy work, requiring almost constant physical activity. Stooping, bending, reaching, climbing, and crouching are frequently required, to install pans in vehicles and equipment, or to clean, paint, or polish the interior and exterior structural sections or accessories.

Depending on both the physical structure of the institution and the duties involved in their jobs, Transportation Equipment Maintenance Workers may work indoors, in maintenance shops or hangar-like display structures, or outdoors, where many pieces of large equipment must be displayed.

WHERE TO FIND THESE JOBS

Transportation equipment is exhibited by many different kinds of institutions located in metropolitan, suburban, and rural areas all over the country. Most of these specialize in one broad field of transportation, land, water, or air. They may be as large as a New England, simulated 18th century seaport where numerous whaling ships and other vessels are displayed, or as small as the many antique auto museums operated by commercial enterprises. They may display only transportation equipment or incorporate it, with other items, into a setting that recreates a particular period of history, geographical area, or kind of technology. These institutions may be commercially or publicly operated, or may be maintained by the Air Force, Navy, or another of the armed forces.

OPPORTUNITIES FOR EMPLOYMENT AND PROMOTION

Both part-time and full-time work are available in this field. Opportunities for part-time jobs are especially good with smaller museums, which either cannot afford to hire full-time maintenance workers or do not own enough vehicles to warrant their employment. Both students and retired workers, if they have the interest and ability to perform this kind of work, can frequently sell themselves to small transportation museums as maintenance workers. Opportunities for full-time work are most numerous at larger institutions, especially those that concentrate their display presentations only on transportation equipment.

In museums operated by branches of the armed forces most work of this kind is done by enlisted personnel, although there may be a few openings for qualified civilians.

The increased participation of museums and similar institutions in government programs such as CETA should permit more hiring of workers in jobs such as these.

These workers may advance to supervisory positions in both large and small establishments or to specialty jobs in the larger institutions. This kind of work also provides good preparation for non-museum work in the areas of construction or crafts.

ZOO VETERINARIAN

OCCUPATIONAL STATEMENT

Maintains zoo veterinary clinic and plans, supervises, and participates in all phases of health care program for zoo animal collection: Establishes and conducts effective quarantine and testing procedures for all incoming animals, to assure health of collection, prevent spread of disease, and comply with government regulations. Conducts regularly scheduled immunization and preventive care program to maintain health of animals and guard against spread of communicable diseases. Provides immediate medical attention to diseased or traumatized animals. Participates with other personnel in planning and executing zoo nutrition and reproduction programs for all animals in collection. Develops special programs, based on knowledge of animals' native habitats and instincts, to encourage reproduction among animals designated as belonging to endangered species Participates in employee training in handling and care of animals in collection. Conducts post mortem studies and analyses. Develops and supervises maintenance of medical record system. May conduct or participate in research concerned with animal health, conservation and management of wildlife, or related subjects.

EDUCATION, TRAINING, AND EXPERIENCE

The Zoo Veterinarian must be a graduate of one of the 20 or so universities in the country that grant the degree of doctor of veterinary medicine. Such a degree requires 2 years of undergraduate pre-veterinary study and 4 years in graduate school. There is no internship required to practice veterinary medicine so, conceivably, an inexperienced recent graduate could be hired as a Zoo Veterinarian. However, most establishments require that these workers have at least 2 years of experience, and prefer that they have knowledge of the special preventive and therapeutic treatment required for exotic animals. A number of government agencies enforce laws related to the importation and preservation of zoo animals: The Animal and Plant Health Inspection Service (APHIS) of the U.S. Department of Agriculture; the U.S. Department of Commerce's National Marine Fisheries Service and National Oceanic and Atmospheric Administration; the Department of the Interior's Fish and Wildlife Service and Federal Wildlife Permit Office, as well as the U.S. Customs Service. The veterinarian who works for a zoo or aquarium should be knowledgeable about laws enforced by these agencies in order to carry out the institution's health care program in compliance with their regulations.

HELPFUL PERSONAL CHARACTERISTICS

Persons interested in becoming Zoo Veterinarians should have, first of all, the intelligence and diligence needed to complete the required educational course, which includes numerous physical and biological science subjects in addition to extensive laboratory work.

Like all members of the medical profession, veterinarians should be interested in doing work of a scientific and technical nature, should be capable of making valid judgments on the basis of both sensory and factual data, and should have the spatial and form perception and manual dexterity needed to perform surgery.

In addition to all of the above qualities, Zoo Veterinarians should also be able to apply their medical knowledge to the development of methods of encouraging captive animals to mate, to plan diets that supply the nutritional needs of a wide variety of animals, and to work with other professionals on research projects.

PHYSICAL DEMANDS AND ENVIRONMENTAL CONDITIONS

This work is more physically demanding than that of veterinarians in general practice. Zoo Veterinarians frequently tour the zoo to observe animals in their quarters and to administer injections. At times, they must work with other employees to subdue animals during treatment, or to move them from one area to another. They may use dart guns to shoot tranquilizing drugs into the animal's bloodstream, rendering it immobile and ready for treatment or movement; at other times, the animal may be lured into a squeeze cage (a barred enclosure with panels that can be constricted to force the animal into a position from which it cannot escape or attack). Some animals must be bound with rope to make treatment possible; fortunately, most large animals can be treated in their quarters, so it is seldom necessary to move animals such as lions, elephants, or walruses very long distances. However, the Zoo Veterinarian should have the physical strength and agility needed to work with others to perform such tasks when necessary.

WHERE TO FIND THESE JOBS

Most zoos and aquariums employ full-time veterinarians. Some of the larger establishments hire two or more persons for such jobs.

Veterinarians in private practice may be hired as part-time workers or consultants by smaller zoos which do not need the services of a full-time worker, or by larger zoos whose veterinarians sometimes require assistance.

OPPORTUNITIES FOR EMPLOYMENT AND PROMOTION

There are usually a few openings for Zoo Veterinarians created as the result of incumbents leaving their positions for one reason or another. Persons interested in becoming veterinarians and who think that they would enjoy working with zoo animals may obtain additional information about hiring requirements and job opportunities by writing to the American Association of Zoo Veterinarians.

Many Zoo Veterinarians may become Directors of the zoos where they have been employed. Except for this possibility, there is little opportunity for advancement from this job.

Veterinarians currently operating a private practice can often make arrangements to work for a zoo on a part-time or consultant basis.

LEARNING OPPORTUNITIES

No evaluations have been made of any of the training facilities listed, and the listing of a facility does not in any way represent an endorsement or recommendation of any of its programs. The list is a compilation, without comment, of museum training opportunities known to the publisher at the time of printing.

The following schools and museums have offered museum-related studies. It is suggested that you write to them and request their current training opportunities.

John C. Calhoun State Community College
Art Gallery
Box 2216
Decatur AL 35602

Division of State Museums
395 Whittier Street
Juneau AK 99801

Arizona State University
Dept. of Anthropology/Museum Studies Program
Tempe AZ 85287

University of Arkansas
University Museum
Fayetteville AR 72701

California State University, Chico
Museum of Anthropology
Chico CA 95929

Denver Museum of Natural History
City Park
Denver CO 80205

Yale University Art Gallery
Curator of American Decorative Arts
2006 Yale Station
New Haven CT 06520

University of Delaware
301 Old College
Newark DE 19716

Museum Studies Program
Academic Center, T215
The George Washington University
Washington DC 20006

University of Florida
Florida State Museum
Gainesville FL 32611

High Museum Of Art
Museum Resource Center
1280 Peachtree Street, N.E.
Atlanta GA 30309

Bernice Pauahi Bishop Museum/ Pacific Regional Conservation Center
Dept. of Education
P.O. Box 19000-A
Honolulu HI 96819

Idaho Museum of Natural History
Idaho State University
Box 8096
Pocatello ID 83209

Southern Illinois University
University Museum
Carbondale IL 62901

Vincennes University
Beless Gymnasium
Vincennes IN

Museum of Natural History
University of Iowa
10 Macbride Hall
Iowa City IA 52240

Kansas State University
Dept. of Clothing, Textiles, and
   Interior Design
Justin Hall
Manhattan KS 66506

University of Kentucky Art Museum
Rose and Euclid Streets
Lexington KY 40606

Louisiana State Museum
P.O. Box 2458
New Orleans LA 70176

Maine State Museum
State House Station 83
Augusta ME 04333

Goucher College
Historic Preservation Program
Towson MD 21204

Arnold Arboretum of Harvard University
The Arborway
Jamaica Plain MA 02130

Center for Cultural and Natural History
Central Michigan University
124 Rowe Hall
Mount Pleasant MI 48859

University of Minnesota
Dept. of Art History
108 Jones Hall
27 Pleasant Street, S.E.
Minneapolis MN 55455

University of Mississippi
Dept. of Art
Fine Arts Center
University MS 38677

University of Missouri-Kansas City
Dept. of History
203 Cockfaire Hall
Kansas City MO 64110

University of Nebraska-Lincoln
Office of Experiential Education
College of Arts and Sciences
Lincoln NE 68588

Nevada State Museum
Capitol Complex
Carson City NV 89710

Science Center of New Hampshire
P.O. Box 173
Holderness NH 03245

Kean College of New Jersey
Fine Arts Dept.
Morris Avenue
Union NJ 07083

Miles Museum
Eastern New Mexico University
Box 2029
Portales NM 88130

Regional Conference of
  Historical Agencies
314 East Seneca Street
Manlius NY 13104

North Carolina State University
Dept. of History
Raleigh NC 27695

North Dakota State University
Dept. of History
Fargo ND 58105

Miami University
Dept. of Sociology and
  Anthropology
Harrison Hall
Oxford OH 45056

University of Oklahoma
1700 Asp Avenue
Suite 226
Norman OK 73037

Museum of Art
University of Oregon
Eugene OR 97403

Pennsylvania State University
School of Visual Arts
270 Chambers Building
University Park PA 16802

Roger Williams College
Historic Preservation Program
Old Ferry Road
Bristol RI 02809

McKissick Museum
University of South Carolina
Columbia SC 29208

South Dakota State University
South Dakota Memorial Art
  Center
Brookings SD 57007

University of Tennessee
Art and Architecture Gallery
1715 Volunteer Bldg..
Knoxville TN 37996

University of Texas at Austin
Dept. of Anthropology
Austin TX 78712

Hogle Zoological Garden
P.O. Box 8475
Salt Lake City UT 84108

Shelburne Museum
Shelburne VT 05482

Sawhill Gallery and Fine Arts
  Collection
James Madison University
Dept. of Art
Harrisonburg VA 22807

University of Washington
Dept. of Anthropology
Seattle WA 98195

United States Dept. of the
Interior
National Park Service
Stephen T. Mather Training
Center
P.O. Box 77
Harpers Ferry WV 25425

Milwaukee Museum/University
of Wisconsin-Milwaukee
Dept. of Anthropology
University of Wisconsin-
Milwaukee
Milwaukee WI 53201

RECOMMENDED READING

The American Association of Museums publishes a monthly dispatch called *Aviso*. This bulletin lists employment opportunities throughout the United States. For subscription information write to:

AVISO
AMERICAN ASSOCIATION of MUSEUMS
1225 EYE STREET N.W.
SUITE 200
WASHINGTON DC 20005

INDEX BY JOB TITLE

ANIMAL KEEPER 1

ANIMAL KEEPER, HEAD 3

ANIMAL NURSE 5

ANIMAL TRAINER 6

AQUARIST 9

ARCHEOLOGICAL ASSISTANT 10

ARCHIVIST 13

ART CONSERVATOR 16

AUDIOVISUAL TECHNICIAN 18

COMMISSARY ASSISTANT 20

CRAFT CENTER DIRECTOR 21

CRAFT DEMONSTRATOR 23

CURATOR 26

DEVELOPMENT DIRECTOR 28

DIRECTOR 30

DIRECTOR, ARTS-AND-HUMANITIES COUNCIL 31

DIRECTOR, EDUCATION 35

EDUCATIONAL RESOURCE COORDINATOR 37

EXHIBIT ARTIST 39

EXHIBIT BUILDER 41

EXHIBIT DESIGNER 44

FINE ARTS PACKER 46

FURNITURE RESTORER 48

GARDEN WORKER 51

GROUNDSKEEPER, INDUSTRIAL-COMMERCIAL 53

GROUNDSKEEPER, PARKS AND GROUNDS 55

GUARD, MUSEUM 57

GUIDE, ESTABLISHMENT 59

HERBARIUM WORKER 61

HISTORIC SITE ADMINISTRATOR 63

INSTALLER 66

LABORATORY ASSISTANT, ZOO 68

LANDSCAPE ARCHITECT 69

LIBRARIAN, SPECIAL LIBRARY 71

LIBRARY ASSISTANT 73

MANAGER, RETAIL STORE 75

MEMBERSHIP SECRETARY 77

MUSEUM ATTENDANT 78

MUSEUM INTERN 80

MUSEUM TECHNICIAN 82

PARK AID 84

PARK RANGER 86

PARK SUPERINTENDENT 88

PLANETARIUM TECHNICIAN 90

PLANT BREEDER 93

PLANT PROPAGATOR 95

RECREATION-FACILITY ATTENDANT 97

REGISTRAR 99

REGISTRAR, MUSEUM 101

RESEARCH ASSOCIATE 103

RESTORER, CERAMIC 105

RESTORER, LACE AND TEXTILES 107

RESTORER, PAPER AND PRINTS 109

RESTORER, PAINTINGS 112

SALESPERSON, GENERAL MERCHANDISE 114

SCHEDULER 116

SECURITY CHIEF, MUSEUM 117

SUPERINTENDENT, HORTICULTURE 119

TAXIDERMIST 121

TEACHER 123

TRANSPORTATION EQUIPMENT MAINTENANCE WORKER 125

ZOO VETERINARIAN 128

ORDER FORM

YES, I want _____ copies of MUSEUM JOBS FROM A–Z at $9.95 each plus $2 shipping per book. (Florida residents, please add 60¢ sales tax.) Canadian orders must be accompanied by a postal money order in U.S. funds. Allow 30 days for delivery.

_____ Check or money order enclosed

Name _____ Phone _____

Address _____

City/State/Zip _____

Check your leading bookstore.

Please make your check payable and return to:

Batax Museum Publishing
2051 Wheeler Lane
Jacksonville, FL 32259